# art+quilt

## Design Principles and Creativity Exercises

*Lyric Kinard*

INTERWEAVE®
interweavestore.com

Editor, Linda Turner Griepentrog
Cover design, Connie Poole
Interior design, Anne Shannon
Photography, Larry Stein, unless otherwise noted
Production, Katherine Jackson

Interweave Press LLC
201 East Fourth Street
Loveland, CO 80537-5655
interweavestore.com

Printed in China by Asia Pacific Offset.

Library of Congress Cataloging-in-Publication Data
Kinard, Lyric.
Art + quilt : design principles and creativity exercises / Lyric Kinard.
      p. cm.
Includes bibliographical references and index.
ISBN 978-1-59668-106-4 (pbk.)
1. Quilting. 2. Art quilts. I. Title.
TT835.K496 2009
746.46'041--dc22
                    2009008796

10 9 8 7 6 5 4 3 2 1

# Dedication

*To Marcel, the love of my life, who has encouraged
and fully supported me from the beginning.
And to my children, who have, of necessity, learned to
be independent and to be patient with frozen dinners.*

# Acknowledgments

*Heartfelt thanks to the Beetweens—
the bee that brought me to the quilt world.*

*Thanks also to Patricia Bolton who pushed, prodded,
and patiently waited, until I finally said "Okay! Okay!
I'll write a book."*

*Thanks also to Haven and Lindy, two sets of welcome
hands in the studio when looming deadlines threatened
to overwhelm. And my undying thanks to the LeBlancs
for their timely proofreading and wonderfully nitpicky
questions before I turned in the manuscript!*

*—Lyric*

# Contents

## How to Use this Book

This book is by no means a comprehensive tome and will not teach you everything you need to know about art. It will, I hope, give you a solid foundation from which to spring and give you direction for further study. It will give you the tools, if you are willing to take the time to learn to use them.

The exercises in this book will help you understand the elements and principles that make up the visual language of art. You will learn to see the world the way an artist sees it. When you are actively looking for good design, searching for the building blocks of art everywhere you look, you will find them all around you and make them a part of your visual vocabulary.

If you are full of confidence and are ready to dive in, I suggest you skip straight to chapter two. Read about each element and then work through the exercises. However, if you've ever uttered the words "I'm not creative," take time to read the first chapter—it's one big pep talk as I strive to convince you that you really can be an artist if you have the desire.

## Why Art?

Why is it that we love art? Why do we need it? What draws us to a flat plane of color, shape, and line and gives it meaning in our lives?

As we view art, we look through a window into the artist's mind. Sometimes we see a depiction of all they find beautiful. Sometimes we can relate to the pain, anger, or confusion we see there. The artist's work draws us in and tells us something about ourselves. Each of us looks at the world differently yet we all long to be validated, to find someone else who sees the world as we do. Art is a direct form of communication—soul to soul, between artist and viewer.

# CHAPTER ONE

# AN INTRODUCTION:
## Getting Ready to Create

*"Every child is an artist. The problem is how to remain an artist once he grows up."* —*Pablo Picasso*

This book is the product of the experience I have every time I show my work. Someone, usually a woman, will come up to me and say, "Oh, I don't know how you do it. I don't have a creative bone in my body." If I'm tired and cranky, the first thought that pops into my head is, "So you think I wave a magic wand and this just happens?"

I've learned to take a deep breath, smile, and ask a few questions. "Why do you think that you're not creative?" They'll usually tell me about the time they tried to make a quilt or drawing and how it didn't meet their expectations or the expectations of a critical elementary school teacher. If I have time and they are willing to listen, I ask a few more questions. "Did you try again? Did you take a class or find someone to teach you? How much time have you spent learning and practicing those skills?"

This has become a personal crusade: I firmly believe that everyone is creative in some way, and that if you have the desire and the willingness to learn, you can become an artist. There are technical skills in the world of visual art that can be learned, just as we learn to read or do math. Why do people think that artists are simply born, springing like Athena from the head of Zeus, fully formed and ready to hunt?

Let me explain it another way. Every preschooler I've met experiences joy in painting. They don't look at their work and say, "The nose on that face isn't perfect, I think I'll give up painting." When is it that we lose confidence in our ability to visually interpret the world? Do we hand a five-year-old a copy of Shakespeare's *Romeo and Juliet* and say, "You're just not a reader, you should do something else," when she gives us a blank stare? No! We teach her the letters of the alphabet and the sounds they make. We teach her to put those letters together to make words, then she practices and progresses until years later, she can pick up Shakespeare and not only make sense of it, but enjoy it. If her heart burns in that direction, she might even go on to write beautiful poetry of her own.

Learning the fundamental elements of art and principles of design is just like learning to read and write. These basic building blocks will help you to understand and more fully enjoy the world of art. They will help you get that creative vision out of your head and onto canvas, paper, or fabric. You may have already mastered many sewing and quilting techniques but lack the confidence to create your own original work. It's as though you have perfect penmanship without knowing how to read. It's never too late to learn your "alphabet," put together words, and practice your reading line by line until you can create visual poetry with your fabric and thread. Remember, Athena was born a goddess. We mere mortals must learn our craft one step at a time.

## Open Your Heart and Mind

"Our deepest fear is not that we are inadequate. Our deepest fear is that we are powerful beyond measure. It is our light, not our darkness, that most frightens us. We ask ourselves, who am I to be—brilliant, gorgeous, talented, fabulous? Actually, who are you not to be?" —*Marianne Williamson*

Think of the last time you stood in front of a quilt you admired. What were your thoughts and your emotions? Was your heart touched, your mind awed, and your fingers itchy to try something new? Were you intrigued and inspired? Or perhaps you felt a little jealous of the artist's success? Did your heart sink as an insidious little voice in your head said, "You could never do that." Most of us have felt, at one time or another, that frustrating lack of confidence as we look at work we perceive to be beyond our current ability. Unfortunately, too many of us listen to those negative thoughts and give up. My dearest wish is that you'll give yourself the chance to discover the creativity that I know you possess.

Think for a moment and ask yourself why you say, "I can't" when it comes to the visual arts? Were you ridiculed or told that making art was a waste of time? If so, I am deeply sorry that this happened to you. Words can wound so deeply.

Caryl Bryer Fallert, an artist whom I have long admired and a woman with great generosity of spirit, said something that I have taken to heart. She was speaking of those people who proclaim that their way is the only right way to do a thing—the "rule makers." She asked, "Why do they think what they do? What outcome do they wish to achieve? Is their end goal the same as yours? Do you respect them and their opinion?" I believe her words apply to criticism about our creative endeavors as well. So many things about art are subjective. Every person has an opinion colored by their personal experiences and view of the world. Their likes and dislikes, their goals and ideas, might be entirely different from yours. Your second grade teacher's idea of good art might be perfect coloring within the lines. Is that really your goal?

If you have the desire to make art, make an effort to stop saying, "I can't" and say, "I'll give it a try." Surround yourself with people who support you. Find others who wish to take the journey and walk together on the path to creativity. If your techniques have failed your vision in the past, find classes that will help you learn the skills you need. Be kind to yourself. Give yourself permission to learn one step at a time and to make mistakes along the way. I'll be your cheerleader, encouraging you every step of the way. I know you can do it!

## Falling Down and Getting Back Up

"Many of life's failures are people who did not realize how close they were to success when they gave up." —*Thomas Edison*

*At my son's first hockey lesson, he couldn't even stand up on his skates. The coach took one look at him and said, "Sorry, no." I had misinterpreted "beginning hockey" as beginning skating. It was a painful experience for both of us, but thanks to the encouragement of a good friend, we didn't give up. I asked the coach to give us one week. We found a friend who could teach my son to skate, and he worked and practiced until he got it. Then he kept working and working. The coach even turned the lights on in the rink for a few afternoons so my son could practice. After a week, he could stand up and move, mostly. He was given a second chance. The coach used to tell him, "I don't care how many times you fall down. I only care about how many times you get up!" Now it brings both of us joy to see him speeding along with ease. There is still a long way to go, and we are still enjoying the journey.*

*—Lyric*

# Overcoming Fear
## By Janine Leblanc

*"Given an equal amount of intelligence, timidity will cause a thousand times more problems than audacity."* —*Carl von Clausewitz*

For a longer period than I'd care to admit, I was paralyzed by the fear of making art. I'd compare myself with other artists and be jealous of their awards, books, and productivity. I needed to overcome those feelings and get back to work, but I couldn't seem to get started. There seemed to be countless things that came first—the job, chores, and relationships—and I was having trouble giving myself permission to make art. I realized that my need to make art was important, too, even if it was time-consuming, and some things would be neglected during the process.

To take the pressure off myself to produce finished work, I made pieces with no intention of exhibiting or even showing them to anyone. I found that I didn't have to have all of the answers before I began. I suspended my expectations and began concentrating on experimentation.

It was important to turn off my inner critic—the voice telling me that my ideas weren't any good or that someone smarter and more wonderful had already done that. Such thoughts will drive you crazy. Now, as often as needed, I tell that critic to just go away.

You're the only one who can make your work—it has to come from you. How do you get there? By making art—lots of it. Talking to it, letting it talk back to you and tell you what it needs. Not everyone will like your work, nor will everyone "get it," but that's okay, too. As long as you make art from a genuine place in yourself, you can never go wrong. You may never become rich or famous but, with time and persistence, your voice will find you.

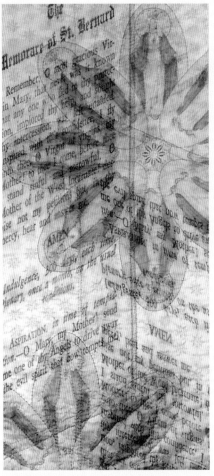

Janine LeBlanc is a trained artist and very talented graphic designer. She has always presented herself professionally, and her artwork has a unique and solid voice. I was truly surprised when I learned that she, like many of us, suffers some hidden insecurities about her artwork.

*Mary Daisy*, 16" × 49" (41 × 124 cm), by Janine LeBlanc

Begin by experimenting with materials and see how they fit together. Have fun with them. Look at these pieces as samples. They're small—take risks with them. Ask yourself if you've taken it far enough or if it needs something else? It takes real courage to risk destroying a piece that's "good enough" in order to make it fabulous. Some of my favorite pieces evolved from experiments that had gone wrong.

As for the fear, I'm still working on it. I'm finding that fear and risk go hand in hand. I'm allowing myself to grow and make the art that I'm meant to make.

## Recognize the Creativity You Already Possess

*"You can't use up creativity. The more you use, the more you have." —Maya Angelou*

When people insist that they're not creative, I simply must disagree. They might not have had success with painting or quiltmaking, but there are so many other ways to be creative. When people cannot express themselves visually, often all they lack are the tools to do so. They haven't been taught to see the world in terms of shape and edge, texture, and value.

Just because you haven't yet made a perfect piece of art to hang on the wall, don't discount your creative abilities. Creativity means using your imagination to solve problems in a new way. Creativity is needed to stick to a tight budget, rearrange your furniture, or solve a problem with a quirky computer. If you can serve a meal with only three ingredients in the fridge, organize an event, solve a customer's problem, or figure out where to stash that new pile of fabric on overflowing shelves, you are creative. There are so many places in your life where you're already manifesting creativity.

Giving yourself credit where it's due is a good start on your journey to being an artist. For centuries, any product that came from a woman's hand was valued only so long as it was utilitarian.

That doesn't mean that the urge to create did not live in a woman's heart. Looking back at our quilting heritage, you will find a plethora of traditional quilts well worthy of any museum wall. You can find complex color studies and compositions with a focal point, balance, and rhythm.

In 1971, Jonathan Holstein and Gail van der Hoof recognized the art and beauty in the quilts they had collected. An exhibition of these utilitarian objects called Abstract Design in American Quilts was hung at the Whitney Museum of American Art in New York City. Showing these quilts on the wall of a museum allowed these

works of art to be recognized by the larger world. It was the beginning of the revitalization of quiltmaking in America. As the creators of those quilts might already have known, creativity and artistic expression can be found in many places other than in a frame on the wall.

Look at the ways you have molded your environment. Pay attention to the things you do. You possess far more creativity than you think. Recognize and acknowledge it. You have the capability to learn and the ability to acquire the tools you need to move your creativity into the world of visual expression.

## My Journey as an Artist

*"Do not go where the path may lead, go instead where there is no path and leave a trail." —Ralph Waldo Emerson*

*Life is interesting. I look over my shoulder and am often amazed at the path I've taken. I never imagined I'd end up working as an artist. I had other hopes, dreams and plans, none of which included five kids and making quilts to hang on the wall. There were great chunks of my life where I worked hard to fulfill the dream of becoming a musician, an architect, or a writer. When I chose to give up those dreams in favor of raising children, I was lost for a while. Every label I had embraced was suddenly gone, and I didn't seem to have any identity other than "mom" (said, of course, in a loud and whining voice). I knew raising children was important, but most of the time it was exhausting, and I floundered around trying to find a little something I could do for my own satisfaction. I finally figured out that I was happiest when I was making things.*

*I began by going to a quilting bee with a good friend just to get out of the house. I enjoyed quiltmaking, as it seemed to be the only thing I ever did that didn't immediately get undone. These women were talented and generous teachers and wonderfully supportive. A few years later I saw my first art quilt. It was as though something opened up inside of me. Quilts could be art? It simply hadn't occurred to me.*

*I began searching for classes that would give me the skills I needed to create the visions that were suddenly floating about in my head. I pulled out my sketchbooks and started jotting down ideas and notes for future projects. I only had bits of time here and there, but I tried to take advantage of them. My progress was very slow because my priorities needed to lie elsewhere. I'll admit I spent years frustrated at having to put my fun stuff on the back burner. I've learned to be patient. Somewhere along the way I blinked, and my little ones were suddenly not so little any more. Time has gone by faster than I could imagine.*

*Now, after working hard and being the recipient of knowledge passed on by many amazing and generous artists, I'm making artwork that I'm not embarrassed to show, teaching a few of the skills that I know, and wonder of wonders, I find myself writing a book. What an amazing journey!*

*—Lyric*

## Yes, You are Creative
### By Laura Cater-Woods

"Creativity belongs to the artist in each of us. To create means to relate. The root meaning of the word art is to fit together and we all do this every day. Not all of us are painters, but we are all artists. Each time that we fit things together we are creating—whether it is to make a loaf of bread, a child, a day." —*Corita Kent*

Creativity is an innate human characteristic. From the moment we take notice of the world we name, explore, discover, and test. We draw conclusions, make relationships between experiences, and form a view of the world. If we are lucky, we're allowed our quiet daydream time. Unfortunately, we are often prodded toward the one right answer and praised for conformity in the interest of helping us "fit in." We may come to the conclusion that creativity exists in others but not in us.

We might think of creativity as a leap of imagination, resulting in new products, new scientific breakthroughs, new art. We may think creative people possess something unique that sets them apart from us. That narrow definition disparages "real-time creativity" and celebrates "multi-stage creativity" as precious and rare.

Every time we solve a problem, from substituting ingredients in a recipe to figuring out a more efficient way to organize an office, we are taking existing information and combining the elements in a new way. This is the essence of creativity. In "real-time creativity" our problem solving is rapid, improvisational, practical, and effective.

"Multi-stage creativity" requires time for the generation of ideas, for sifting and sorting to find possibilities, and time to

*River is Wide,* 9" × 23" (23 × 58 cm), by Laura Cater-Woods

implement and test those possibilities. This is the creativity most of us associate with the arts and sciences, with leaps of imagination and invention.

If we want to expand our creativity and be more intentional in how we use it, we should:

• Cultivate curiosity about the world and learn about a variety of things in addition to our particular field of interest.

• Spend some time each day in solitude. The brain needs "quiet time" to work on the deeper levels.

• Practice "mindfulness." Pay attention to the tasks at hand no matter what they are, giving the brain a chance to work without the distraction of multitasking chatter.

• Learn to consider more than one point of view as being equally valid.

• Create an environment that nourishes and stimulates you.

• Have relationships with people who support you and your creative energies.

• Do you think of yourself as "creative"? If not, change your way of thinking. We live up to, or down to, what we expect of ourselves.

• Build regular time into your life for creative exploration.

• Know that creativity is not a rare quality given only to a few. Creativity is a state of being available to all.

Laura Cater-Woods is a working studio artist with an extensive international exhibition record and numerous awards. In person, I'm impressed not only with her talent, but with her gentle and caring nature. She truly is an encouraging and nurturing teacher and an amazing creativity coach. See her work at cater-woods.com.

## Dream Your Dream

*"We know what we are, but know not what we may be."* —William Shakespeare

What do you want to do, and who do you wish to be? The answers to these questions can make all the difference in moving forward. If you don't know where you are going, then it really doesn't matter which path you take, does it? If you have a destination in mind, your path might take a few unexpected twists and turns, but you will make progress toward your goal. Defining your dreams will help you bring them into reality.

Take a moment to imagine your journey. Begin by shutting the critic that lives in your head in a deep dark closet with a great big lock! Every time a negative thought, doubt, or that whining little "I can't, I'm no good at this" voice tries to sneak in, replace it with thoughts like "I'll give it a try" or "I can learn this." The minute you think "I can't," you are really saying "I choose not to try."

Now, close your eyes and imagine a theater. Empty stage. Black curtains. Spotlight on. No critics. No audience. Place yourself on the stage five years from now. Who are you? What do you look like? What labels or titles have you chosen to embrace? Where are you? What environment have you created? Who is surrounding you and supporting you? What are you doing? Imagine that there are no obstacles, no inhibitions, nothing holding you back. Give yourself permission to dream the most joyful, wildest, and biggest dream you can possibly imagine. We're talking about pure pie-in-the-sky fantasy, completely leaving reality behind. Take the time to examine and flesh out as many details as you can imagine. Think about what is important to you. Enjoy this vision and spend some time with it. Write down as much of your vision as you can.

Now, reset the stage. Place yourself on the stage as you see yourself now. What labels have you accepted? Where are you? What are you doing, and who is surrounding you? Don't judge your current position as good or bad. It is simply one point on your journey's path. There are many experiences that have brought you here and there is still a long way yet to go.

Now, see yourself facing forward on the path that leads to your ideal "future-self" vision. Take one step. Look at your labels. Are there any that you wish to discard, acquire, or mold into a more comfortable fit? Take another step toward your vision. There might be some obvious changes you need to make, such as scheduling time to work and finding a place to do it. There might be some mountains to climb. Some parts of your vision might be separated from the present by a seemingly impenetrable fog. Don't worry. Every journey includes surprises, detours, and obstacles, but also unforeseen bridges and people who will help you along the way. You only need to take one step at a time.

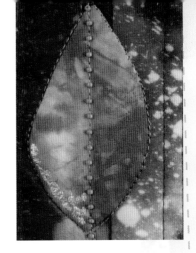

# My Dream

"All our dreams can come true—
if we have the courage to pursue
them." —*Walt Disney*

*One of the classes I took very early in my journey to becoming an artist included an interesting exercise. I didn't even know I wanted to be an artist at the time. I had just made the decision to start a family rather than attend graduate school. I was taking community classes here and there just to stay sane. I vaguely remember sitting with my palms over my eyes, the instructor gently guiding us through a visualization. We imagined our hopes and dreams for the present and the future. I imagined myself pregnant and standing at my drafting table in a beautiful studio with floor to ceiling windows.*

*Life moved on, and I forgot all about that class until almost five years later. I had a startling and vivid flash of memory while standing at my drafting table working on a quilt. I now had two children and had found a medium that allowed for the constant interruptions that come with motherhood. I had spent my entire pregnancies terribly sick, most definitely NOT standing at the table, and the "studio" was shared with the baby's crib, but there I was, living my dream. It came as something of a shock to realize that I had envisioned this outcome and arrived at my destination. Now I try to make it a regular habit to dream my goals and write them down. I am constantly surprised at the serendipity that brings about their fruition.*

*—Lyric*

# The Freedom to be Creative
## By Carter Smith

> "You are the creator; give your art the freedom to choose its path. Pay attention, you will see this path. Pay attention, your art will speak to you. Pay attention, and your art will speak to others."
>
> —A. Wayne Hooker

There is a force that connects all of us to each other. Some people call it the collective conscience. It is the ultimate creative place where we are most connected to ourselves. If I am to teach you, my highest goal is to connect you to yourself, to help you find that place within you where all is connected. Connecting to your dreams on a conscious level is the first step toward implementing that power into the world of reality. When I work and I let go, the creative process is an external force I am facilitating. In the end, it is really not about me. It is above me, and around me, and through me.

You can find that connected place within you by letting go and being unafraid of failure. To find it, you must be willing to be lost. If you always know where you are, you will never know where you can be.

If we can create our dreams, then our dreams can create us. Those who say that they are not creative, for the most part dream. Those dreams come through them, and from them, and reflect who they are.

The best way to realize your dreams is to connect to them. The most fertile time for ideas is in the transition between the conscious and subconscious. Keep a journal by your bedside and when you wake up with an inspiration, write it down. Acknowledging and holding onto these thoughts as they pass through you will help them come more easily and often. In the morning when you look at your notes or drawings, you will remember your ideas and can then elaborate on each thought. Making those initial connections is most important. The more you connect, the easier it is.

Carter Smith is a renowned shibori artist whose wearable art is highly sought after. He is also a very generous and caring individual who thinks deeply about our connectedness to each other and to the universe. He's an example of one who has truly opened himself to fearless creative exploration. See his work at shibori.com.

*Anemone Garden*, 45" × 18' (114 × 549 cm), by Carter Smith

## Inspiration vs Perspiration

*"Don't wait for inspiration. It comes while working."* —Henri Matisse

An artist learns one step at a time. She learns to look carefully and see shapes and edges and textures, to draw and use color in her own unique way. She spends hundreds of hours practicing and developing her own vision and voice. She will learn techniques, take courses, and learn from people she admires. She reads, looks, watches, and asks questions. Most of all, she spends time creating art, a lot of it.

If you really want to develop as an artist, you need to be willing to give yourself time to learn and grow from your efforts, and to acquire the techniques you need to make your vision come to life. If you're saying "I can't" because you gave it one try and compared your failure to the success of someone who has put a lot of effort into learning what they do, then you are lying to yourself.

Artists don't show you their failures, only their successes. I've got plenty of ugly quilts that either didn't get finished or were given away to charities. I certainly don't send them out to galleries.

It takes work to express yourself as an artist. How often do we look at a finished piece by a master and envy their creative genius, forgetting everything it took to climb to that level? If you tried to make something and it didn't turn out like you had hoped, did you try again or did you give up? Did you analyze what went wrong and seek to improve your skills? Are you comparing your talent to someone who has dedicated thousands of hours to learning and practicing her art? Not every artist was able to draw from the moment a pencil was placed in her hands. A successful artist will have a willingness to take chances and try new things, as well as a determination to work hard and learn from failure.

If you want to become an artist, you will need to make lots and lots of art, both good and bad. There might be some parts of the process that are boring or difficult. There will be frustrations and downfalls. If you never fail, it simply means that you aren't moving out of your comfort zone and learning anything new.

Give yourself permission to try something new without being perfect the first time. Mistakes will allow you to pursue other options. Think of them as design opportunities. I look at a failure and analyze what I did wrong. I learn everything I can from it and then stick it in a notebook or simply put it away. It has served its purpose, and now I can move on.

## Don't Wait for the Muse

*"Even though it may only take one hour to produce a great work of art, there are years of nurtured vision and feeling in every stroke."* —Susan Easton Burns

*I had several jobs in my past life as a musician. Friends often thought those jobs were glamorous and lucrative. When I looked at it, I saw a few hours of well-paid and very rewarding performances, preceded by years of lessons and hundreds of hours of practice, auditions, and rehearsals. A musician must spend years learning scales and techniques. He fixes wrong notes, listens, and plays until the structure of the music becomes second nature and he can move easily in and around notes and rhythms to create something new and spontaneous. He doesn't wait until he has a great idea to pick up his horn and play it. A dancer spends years training and developing her body into a finely honed tool that will allow her to gracefully leap and move and express herself on the stage. An athlete sweats and works and practices endless hours for that one moment of winning glory. It takes hard work, and lots of it, to become an artist.*

*—Lyric*

## Doing the Work
### By Hollis Chatelain

*"Boldness has genius, power, and magic.
Engage, and the mind grows heated.
Begin, and the work will be completed."*
—*Johann Wolfgang von Goethe*

There is a misconception that artists must be talented to succeed. I believe that passionate artists are much more likely to succeed than talented artists. A passionate artist will create every day. Creating becomes a need, and the love of doing it compels an artist to work every day.

I've been working professionally as an artist since 1976. When people tell me that I am talented, my response is "It is a sad situation if you do something eight hours a day for thirty-two years without improvement." I probably would have been voted as "the least likely to succeed" in college. I don't believe I was talented, but I was passionate. Passionate enough to continue taking drawing classes or setting up drawing groups as I moved from one country to another. When I couldn't find other artists, I bought books or magazines with lessons on drawing, color, or design in them and did the lessons on my own. I have worked in many art forms, from photography to toy design, and accepted any job that entailed creating. Doing art every single day has been a driving force in my life.

Since being a full-time artist is so time consuming, I sometimes have to make an effort to just focus on my work and not get involved in too other many things. I volunteer quite a bit but don't spread myself too thin. Dividing my time between creating challenging new quilts, spending time with people that inspire me, volunteering, and marketing my work helps me to mature as an artist and remain enthusiastic about my textile art.

*Hope For Our World*, 82" × 82" (208 × 208 cm), by Hollis Chatelain

Hollis Chatelain is an internationally known textile artist. When her husband gave up his career with humanitarian organizations in Africa and the family moved to the United States, they took a leap of faith and threw their support entirely behind Hollis's career. She has supported her family with her artwork, putting three children through college with hard work, passion, and willingness to take risks. See her work at hollisart.com

# No Excuses

"The studio is less important than other things, like the burning desire to paint. If you don't have this disease, you can't catch it from a nice studio." —*Warren Criswell*

There are many roadblocks you can put up in your own way. Two of the most common excuses I've heard are "no time" and "no space." I am the mother of five children. I'm involved in my children's activities, my church, and my community. I have almost no spare time, but I have learned to leave the TV off and to limit my computer time. I take my sketchbook and a small "to-go" project everywhere. It's amazing how much work gets done in these little "lost" bits of time.

I've learned that you don't need a large space to work with textiles. For a few years, I sewed standing up at a corner of the kitchen counter. It was too high for the little ones to reach. I could leave my projects out and take a stitch here and a stitch there. I moved up a bit at a time—first to a table in the nursery, then a closet, then a shared office. Now, years later, I am blessed with my own studio. Instead of a door I have a baby gate so I can keep an eye on the little ones, and they can find me when they need me. They can't come in, but we do often share a rousing game of "throw toys at mommy while she sews." It does help to have some space, no matter how small, dedicated to your artwork. Then you can leave it out and spend your few minutes of time working rather than setting up. Use your creativity and find a corner to claim as your own.

Keep in mind that there are times when other things in your life must take priority over the production of your art. Don't beat yourself up if now really isn't the time for you to pursue this dream. There truly is a season for every purpose in your life. There have been years in which I have let my art lie fallow while I concentrated on other, more immediately important areas in my life. I don't, however, let that field be trampled or sold off for a parking lot. Often a farmer plants a nitrogen-fixing crop into that fallow field and tills it into the soil at the end of the season, adding nutrients for the upcoming crop. I kept a sketchbook and stacks of art and technique books on hand while I nursed my babies. I doodled ideas and filled my brain a bit at a time so that when I was once again able to take the time to make art, there were plenty of ideas to choose from. I was ready to burst full-flowered from the ground because I had nourished and replenished the soil of my creativity.

—*Lyric*

Are you ready now? Have you silenced the critic, dreamed your goals, found your creativity, and are determined to do the work? Are you ready to learn the alphabet and language of art? Great! Let's go!

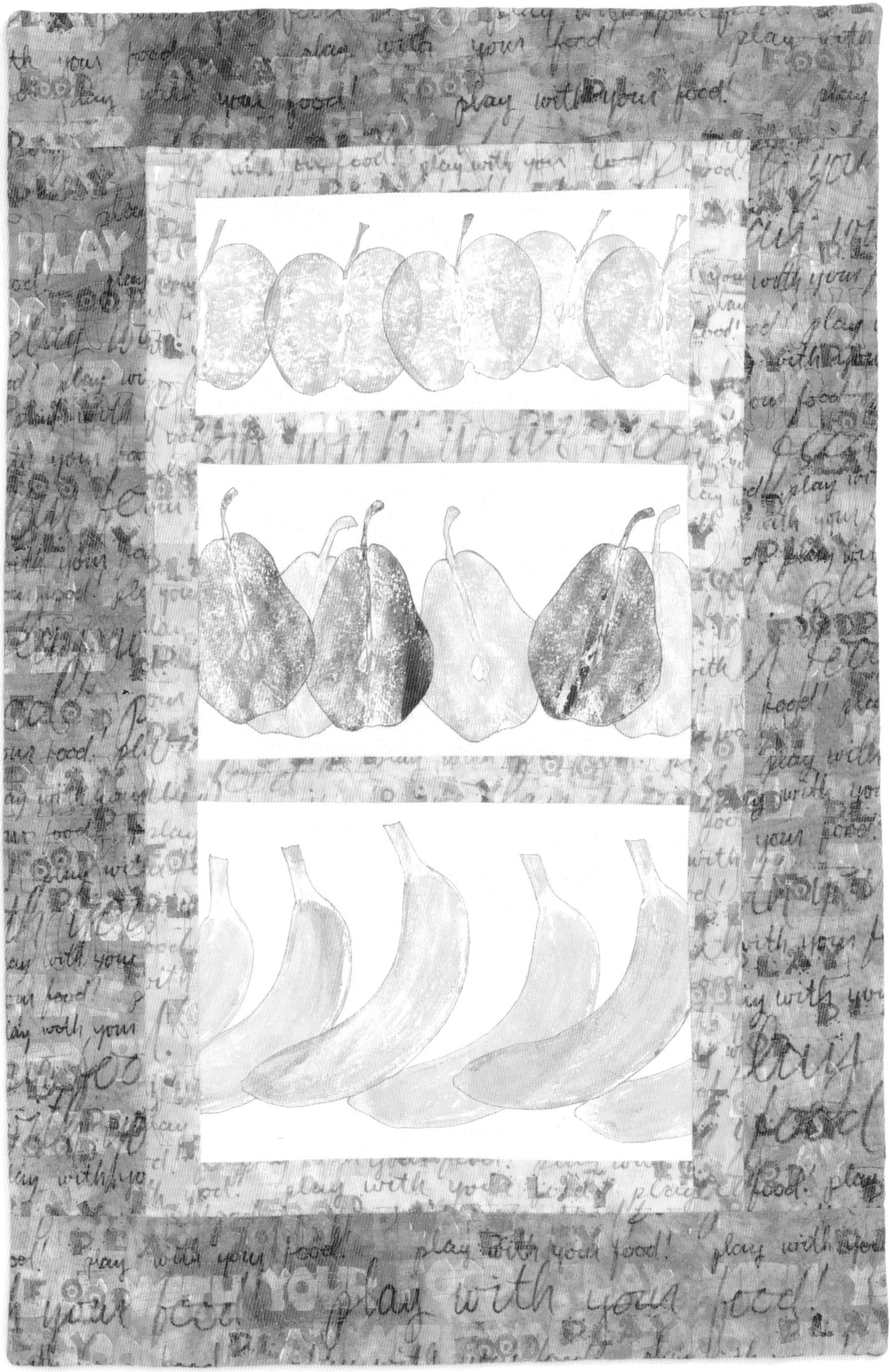
play with your food!

# CHAPTER TWO

# LEARNING THE ALPHABET:
## The Elements of Art

In the next two chapters, we'll work up from the sounds and shapes of letters (the elements), to the combinations that make words and sentences (the principles of art). You'll be given the tools for your belt and shown how to use them. How wonderful it is to be able to turn a visual image into a message that interprets and conveys your own vision and imagination so that others can share and understand it.

## Introduction to Design Elements

When a child is introduced to the wonderful world of written language, she already knows the sounds of speech. She hears words every day and knows what they mean. She enjoys the poetry of lyrics set to music. What she doesn't yet have is the ability to interpret the shapes and meanings of letters. Do you remember the amazing world that opened up to you when you learned to read and write? Suddenly you had the power to enter the imagination of an author, sharing their vision through the words in a book.

The elements of art are the letters of the alphabet, the basic building blocks used in the visual language. You and I can already see the world around us. We see color and shape, darkness and light. We enjoy looking at art and illustrations. We understand what is being sold to us when we look at an advertisement. What an amazing thing it is to learn the alphabet of the visual world, to gain a deeper understanding of what we see, of how the elements work together. As we learn the basic principles of art and design, we learn to assign meaning to these visual tools and to use them purposefully in our own creations.

## Before we begin

As you work your way through the book, I encourage you to read about and absorb each concept until you feel you have a basic understanding of it. Then, as we discussed in chapter one, practice and gain experience to make these tools your own.

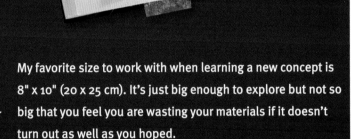

## How to do the *Exercises*

I'm offering you some exercises to help master each concept. Give yourself time and permission to play. The pieces you make don't have to be useful for anything other than the learning process. When you are concentrating on learning instead of making masterpieces, even your mistakes become valuable. If you have trouble and find yourself worrying about making mistakes, set a timer for ten minutes and just do the exercise. Remember, we are the luckiest people in the world to be able to play with fabric and make art.

My favorite size to work with when learning a new concept is 8" x 10" (20 x 25 cm). It's just big enough to explore but not so big that you feel you are wasting your materials if it doesn't turn out as well as you hoped.

Place each exercise or project in a binder with clear page protectors when it is complete. Write on the back of the piece what you were studying, what your thoughts were, how you think you succeeded, and what you might have learned from any mistakes you made. If you absolutely adore the piece you made and want to finish it and hang it on the wall, great! Scan it or take a picture of it and place that in your notebook instead of the original.

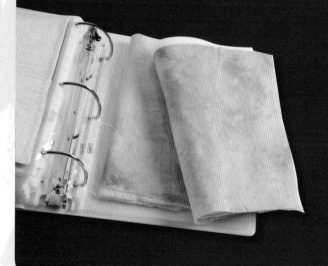

# Materials

You probably have most of the items on hand that you'll need for these exercises. If expensive materials intimidate you, use cheap ones while you practice and get to the good stuff as soon as you can. I find that using beautiful materials draws me to do the work. I love the deep black of a Faber-Castell Artist pen and the heavy, smooth paper of a hard-cover sketchbook. Beautiful fabric just begs me to use it. I got over the fear of cutting into my favorite fabrics when I realized that someone might sell them for pennies at a yard sale after I die! I'd rather enjoy them now.

## Sketchbooks and Cameras

You'll find that there is great value in the physical act of drawing what your eyes see. When you do exercises in a sketchbook, don't worry about your drawing ability. No matter how bad you think you are, you cannot improve unless you practice. Think about one concept and one detail at a time. Take written notes as well as visual ones.

To break up the landscape around you into more manageable bite-size pieces, make yourself a "window" tool out of a piece of card stock or buy a precut 5" x 7" (12.5 x 18 cm) picture-frame mat. Make sure your window opening has the same length/width ratio as your sketchbook. Look through your window tool and concentrate on what you see there. Use a soft sketching pencil or a black-ink pen. I find that there is something liberating about the inability to erase. Take a deep breath and go for it! If you make a mess, simply turn the page and start over. Think of your sketchbook as a tool rather than a precious object and use it up without hesitation.

A digital camera can also be a wonderful tool. It can frame your view and quickly capture compositions, values, and textures. Beware, however, that photographs lie! What your camera captures is never exactly what your mind sees. Colors in a print are never quite the same, electrical wires appear out of nowhere, and odd things sprout from people's heads. When you're gathering inspiration, use your camera as a reference tool. Don't slavishly follow what you see in the print.

Use your camera together with your sketchbook, rather than as a replacement for it. The act of drawing will help you see details and understand composition in a way that you cannot learn by clicking the camera shutter alone. Again, these are learning exercises, not final exams. Time your drawings in one-, five-, and ten-minute increments so you don't get too caught up in making them "perfect." Just learn about the element at hand and move on. You CAN do it. Some concepts and skills might come easily and naturally to you, some might be a bit of a struggle. This is a natural and normal part of the learning process all artists go through. Keep trying, learning from your mistakes, and resolve to try again until you feel you understand the concept.

# The Order Elements for
## the Textile Artist

In most beginning art courses, the order in which you study the basic elements is line, shape, and then texture. Color, in all its glorious complexity, can occupy an entire course by itself, no matter what medium you choose. When you are working with a pencil or a brush, this approach makes sense. You draw a line, close it to make a shape, and then fill it with texture. As quilt artists we work mainly in the opposite direction. We choose the texture of our fabric, cut out shapes, then add line with stitching and thread. The wonderful thing about our medium is that the elements are richly layered and interconnected. A shape cut out of fabric might already have printed lines and visual textures. Quilting stitches make ridges and valleys of batting and cloth that add another complex layer of texture. Threads and textured cords that embellish the surface of the quilt add lines that enclose and emphasize shapes. Amazing isn't it? The elements blend, overlap, and are as many-layered as the quilt itself.

> ## Texture
> The way something feels to the touch or the visual patterns on a surface.

There is something wonderful about working with cloth. It's a functional object in our everyday existence, clothing us, warming us, and softening many of the surfaces in our homes. Yet, with the skilled touch of an artist's hand, it can be transformed into soul-inspiring fine art, leaving us breathless as we look at a beautiful quilt on the wall. The shapes and colors catch our eye, and as we move closer we're drawn into the details. We're enchanted by complex patterns and layers, by stitched lines and embellishments, and, finally, by the fabric itself. From the day we're born, we are wrapped in cloth and intimately know its touch. The fabric of a quilt provides an immediate connection between artist and viewer. Time after time, I've watched as a visitor

leans in, then reaches out a hand to gently touch the quilts on my wall. I have beautiful paintings and photographs as well, but have yet to see anyone reach out to touch them. It is our personal tactile experience with cloth that draws us into the work. I believe many working artists who have chosen textiles as a medium love it for this quality. We understand and can connect with the feel of a silky-smooth satin and the roughness of coarsely woven linen.

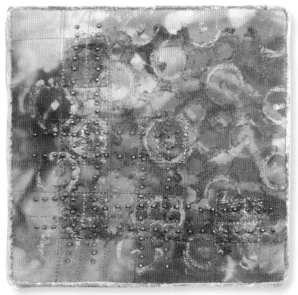

Every visual pattern in the cloth, stitched line, or added bead adds to the texture of an art quilt.

### Tactile Texture

Many times, even before you've chosen a subject for your textile art, you'll choose the texture of your cloth. Tactile texture is the way the cloth feels when you touch it, the difference between satin and burlap. Visual texture is the way the cloth looks, from the printed or woven pattern such as a subtle brocade to a bright and bold Hawaiian print. If you've come from the traditional quilting world, you'll probably have quite a fabric stash. Before the colors ever catch your eye, you've chosen the strength of plainly woven cotton. You know how it stretches across the bias and is stable on the grain. It's both familiar and comfortable to work with. It might be time for you to expand your palette, to broaden your variety of textures. Consider the shimmering effects created by the lustrous fibers of silk—so smooth, so cool. Think of the luxurious pile of velvet that absorbs light and is impossible for fingers to resist. What of the warmth and strength of wool that can be steamed into dimensional shapes? Wool can evoke memories of both warmth and softness and roughness and itchiness. As a textile artist, you have an infinite variety of textures to choose from, and each fiber you use will bring its own connotations and characteristics to your artwork.

As you begin to gather your fabric for each new piece of art, think for a moment of how each texture will affect your work. Will the viewer immediately see the weave of the cloth, or is it so smooth and tightly woven that it reflects the light? Can you use those qualities to evoke certain emotions or feelings? Imagine similar compositions executed in solid, plain-woven cottons as opposed to richly brocaded upholstery fabrics. Each will have a different effect, both close up and at a distance. Smooth cottons might give room for more interesting quilting patterns and threads, while the brocade's textural depth will overshadow anything but the heaviest or brightest of quilting threads. Combining fibers such as wool and silk add depth and dimension, simply because of their differing thicknesses. Pieced cottons might appear to be one flat surface. Neither is better than the other—the choice of which textures to use depends entirely on the effect you wish to create.

Don't forget that you can also change the texture of any piece of cloth by manipulating it. It can be scrunched, wrinkled, pleated, folded, felted, or twisted to add interest to your work.

## Visual Texture

Visual texture also comes into play early in the creative process of the textile artist. Fabric comes in an infinite variety of patterns and colors. A large-scale floral print might jump off the shelf and into your stash to sit happily next to a tiny overall pattern and a solid hand-dyed cloth. The patterns printed, painted, and dyed onto our cloth are visual textures that our eyes read and understand in the same way that our fingers feel and understand a tactile texture.

A bold visual texture will automatically become a dominant feature when placed with more subdued prints and solids. What happens if your entire quilt is made of bold prints? Vastly different results are achieved simply by varying the visual texture of the fabric you choose. As you look through your palette of fabric, do you find that you have a leaning toward one kind of visual texture? Could interest be added to your artwork by introducing a broader range of fabric patterns? The change doesn't always have to be drastic. When I use my hand-dyed fabrics, there are often pieces that look almost solid. When placed next to a mottled or printed piece of fabric, the contrast can be quite lively if that's the desired effect. A visually patterned fabric can also add the element of surprise when used in unexpected ways. I enjoy making portraits with patterned and brightly colored batiks rather than solids. Seeing these playful visual textures where we would expect to see smooth skin colors adds interest to the composition.

A second aspect of visual texture is the imitation of a real texture. Can you represent the look and feel of wood or weathered stone with fabric and thread? What about the foam on a wave, lichen on a fallen log, or rust on an old car? These imitated textures can be realistically portrayed or subtly implied. An abstract composition might simply imply the texture of grass through shape and color. In this case, the visual texture of the artwork might mean one thing to the artist and something entirely different to the viewer.

## Gathering Inspiration

Go outside or move to a different environment. Bring your window, sketchbook, and camera. Spend some time finding and recording different textures. Don't worry about drawing perfect representations. An impression is worth just as much.

Get down close to the ground and notice the texture of the pavement, a beetle shell, or a tufted rug. How does the visual texture of that tree change when you move from closeup to far away? As I look at the cypress tree out my window, its needles seem soft and feathery as they swish gently in the wind. I know from experience, however, that if I stick my bare arm into the branches, I'll come away with numerous scratches from the pointed needles and prickly branches. The closeup, actual texture is very different from the distant visual texture. What are some words you would use to describe the visual texture of an upholstered couch or glass vase? Close your eyes and feel things, then write down what those things remind you of.

Think about how you could re-create or suggest those textures with fabric? What kind of fibers and weaves would you like to use? What if you had to use the opposite fiber from your first choice? Could you evoke the feeling of rough pine bark with a smooth silk?

# Recipe for *Composition*

If creating a composition out of the blue for these exercises is intimidating, begin with this simple recipe. Cut four shapes, beginning with three different-size circles and a long rectangle; use those as your main compositional elements. As you grow more confident, try different shapes and sizes and play around with different colors, but remember to concentrate on the element or principle you are learning. If you find yourself worrying about getting it wrong, set a timer for fifteen minutes. Work hard and fast until the timer goes off, then stop. You can go back and stitch into the piece or leave it as it is. Write down what you were working on and what you think you learned, then put your sample in your notebook.

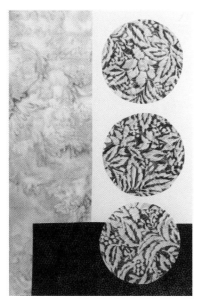

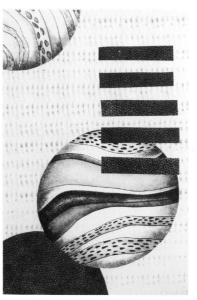

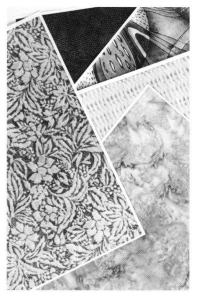

A simple recipe of three circles and a rectangle becomes a pleasing composition after a little playing around.

Both subdued and bold visual textures can be combined for greater interest.

Using photocopies will help you concentrate solely on the visual texture of your materials.

# EXERCISE

## Visual Texture

For this exercise, use black-and-white photocopies of your fabric. You can also scan or take digital pictures of your fabric and print them out in black and white. If you don't have access to these technologies, view your work through a piece of red plastic, such as a report cover, to eliminate the element of color.

1. Find five different fabrics, each with a different visual texture or pattern.

2. Make two page-size black-and-white paper copies of each fabric.

3. Use an 8" x 10" (20 x 25 cm) piece of paper for a background.

4. Cut shapes from the papers and arrange them to achieve a pleasing composition.

5. Use a glue stick to keep things together once you're satisfied with your work.

6. Repeat this exercise several times, varying your work.

Ask Yourself . . .

*What happens if you exchange a large print for a small-scale pattern?*

*A plain white background has no visual texture, how would the composition change with a patterned background?*

*From a distance, how do the patterns read and affect each other?*

*Which is the dominant texture and how could you make a different texture dominant?*

7. Take notes and add this sample to your notebook.

# EXERCISE

## Actual Texture

1. Collect a variety of different fabrics, threads, and embellishments, in neutral, white, or beige.

2. Find as broad a range as possible, from rough burlap to silky satin.

3. Use an 8" x 10" (20 x 25 cm) piece of batting or muslin as a base.

4. Create a composition with these fabrics, concentrating on the use of texture.

5. Feel free to alter the texture of any of your fabrics by scrunching, folding, needlefelting, etc.

Ask Yourself . . .

*How would exchanging rough for smooth fabric affect the composition?*

*How does the light play with each fiber and weave?*

*Which texture catches your eye first; why?*

*What memories or connections do the different fibers bring to mind?*

*Use pins, a glue stick, or fusible web to keep the pieces in place.*

6. Use hand or machine stitches to quilt and/or embroider the piece, adding more texture.

7. Feel free to add any embellishments such as beads, buttons, or cords, always playing with texture.

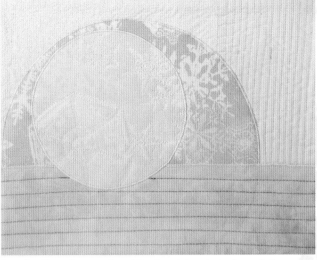

Smooth cottons allow room for quilting threads to gain dominance in the textural scheme of things.

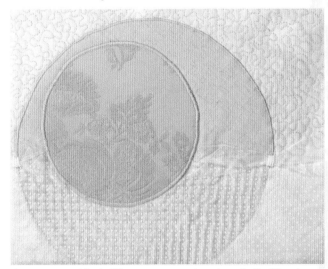

The same composition in different textures can have dramatically different results.

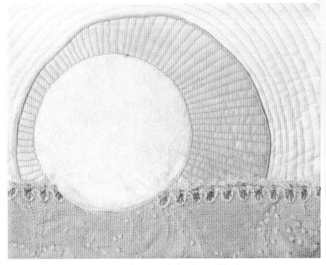

The texture of heavy velvets and jacquards dominate this piece.

The background becomes a dominate shape in this composition.

## Shape

A closed two- or three-dimensional form encased by a line or an edge. A distinct visual unit.

Shape is an element intimately familiar to quilters. Unless we're working whole-cloth, we textile artists must cut out shapes to create our work. The placement of shapes can direct and control where the viewer's eye is first attracted, where it travels next, and where it ends. Think of the circle at the center of a bull's-eye or a large square at the lower portion of a landscape. Both are solid, stable, stationary, and hold your attention. Odd blobs, splatter shapes, and spirals are active and full of movement. Curves tend to move your eye along while straight-edge shapes and right angles can either stop your eye in its tracks or shoot you quickly in a different direction.

It's almost impossible to separate the elements of shape and texture in the quilting world. Our textures are full of shapes and our shapes are full of texture. Traditional quilters choose a block pattern full of repeated shapes, go to their fabric stashes and choose visually textured and patterned cloth. Each piece we cut is a shape and is joined with other pieces to create new and increasingly complex shapes. Quilters choosing fusing or appliqué as their primary construction technique work with floating shapes just like a collage artist. A shape can be abstract or part of a larger object, such as the eye in a face or the petal of a flower.

Shapes, like textures, will summon up memories and associations. Even when viewing purely abstract artwork, we can't help but assign our own meanings to the shapes we see. A circle becomes an apple, a moon, or a face. A triangle becomes a pyramid or an arrow. Look at any piece of abstract art for a minute and very quickly your brain will start making connections to the world around you. It's the way our brains work.

The empty area within the border around your main subject is called negative space and becomes its own shape. It can have an impact on the success of your artwork. Many times we become so focused on the main object we're creating that we forget the background and the important role it plays in our composition. Pay attention as you compose your work and try to integrate your shapes into your backgrounds. It's also possible for a background shape to inadvertently become a dominant element in the artwork.

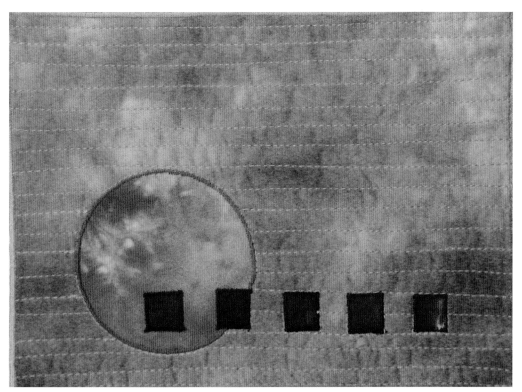

The shapes seem to float on the background.

Adding a few more shapes in neutral colors integrates the main elements with the background.

## Gathering Inspiration

Pick up your sketchbook, window tool, and camera and take a look around. See how houses, cars, and toys are made of many shapes put together. A tree from far away is one shape, while closeup each leaf is a different shape. Look through your window, find an interesting item, and draw the shape of the empty space around the object rather than the object itself. Take pictures of the shapes that make up buildings and landscapes. Use your viewfinder to frame an interesting composition that leads your eye through a thoughtful journey.

Find a picture of a landscape in a book or magazine. Place a piece of tracing paper over your picture and trace the major shapes. Squint a bit so that the details disappear and concentrate only on the major forms and their placement. Trace the border as well, giving the composition boundaries.

Remove the tracing paper and look at your composition. Where do the shapes in the composition lead your eye? How do the shapes relate to each other and the background?

# Contour Drawing

This classic exercise has more to do with learning to see than with drawing. As you learn to observe with a pencil in your hand you will develop an increased ability to draw.

Get a blank piece of paper or sketchbook page ready. Place your pencil in your dominant hand on the lower left corner of your paper. Facing 90 degrees away from the paper, place your other hand in front of you, on the table or in your lap. Rivet your eyes to the lower left side of your wrist and then, very slowly, follow the edges of your hand with your eyes, moving in a clockwise direction. Without looking at the paper, follow the movement of your eyes with your pencil, drawing every edge and detail of what you see. Don't lift the pencil. Don't worry about how weird it's going to turn out. Your brain is learning the artist's way of seeing contours, shapes, lines, and details. Practice the exercise several more times with different objects or with your hand in a different position. Then modify the exercise by moving the paper in front of you. Your eye will still follow the edge of the object, but you can glance at your paper occasionally, or just keep tabs on it with your peripheral vision, to register where your pencil is. Another variation of this exercise is to look through your window tool and draw only the spaces around the object.

Further Reading:
*Drawing on the Right Side of the Brain*, Betty Edwards

MODIFIED CONTOUR DRAWING

"BLIND" CONTOUR DRAWING

Don't worry about how crazy the final result of a blind contour drawing looks. The exercise is about seeing more than it is about drawing.

## EXERCISE

## Shape and Meaning

1. Gather a paper, pencil, and tracing paper.

2. Draw a few simple but familiar shapes, such as a house, couch, baseball bat, or flower.

3. Cut them out and arrange these objects until you have a pleasing composition on an 8" x 10" (20 x 25 cm) background.

4. Use tracing paper to trace your composition.

5. With a second piece of tracing paper, bend, stretch, and change your shapes a bit at a time.

Ask Yourself . . .

How far can you take your changes and still keep the meaning of those shapes?

At what point do the shapes no longer imply the figures you began with?

Can you create a composition where the shape of the background has equal importance to the foreground?

6. Use a piece of 8" x 10" (20 x 25 cm) of muslin and batting as a foundation.

7. Choose several solid fabrics and create an abstract composition based on your tracings.

8. Keep in mind the shape of the background and how your eye moves within the frame.

9. Use pins, a glue stick, or fusible web to keep the pieces in place.

10. Use hand or machine stitches to quilt and/or embroider the piece, emphasizing shape.

11. Feel free to add any embellishments as long as they continue the study of shape.

A detail of the leaf becomes an abstract form.

A pointed oval becomes a leaf with a few modifications.

# EXERCISE

## Shape: Active vs Stationary

1. Use a piece of 8" x 10" (20 x 25 cm) muslin or batting as a foundation.

2. Choose a dark, solid fabric.

3. Cut out several shapes and arrange them on your base.

4. Try to create a very active composition.

Ask Yourself . . .

*What shape attracts your eye first?*

*How does the placement of the shapes affect the movement of your eyes?*

*What shape is the background?*

*Does it have equal or less importance than the foreground shapes?*

5. Use pins, a glue stick, or fusible web to keep the pieces in place.

6. Use hand or machine stitches to quilt and/or embroider the piece, emphasizing shape.

7. Feel free to add any embellishments as long as they continue the study of shape.

8. Repeat the exercise with the same fabric, this time creating a still and calm composition.

Pointed and spiraling shapes are very active in this composition.

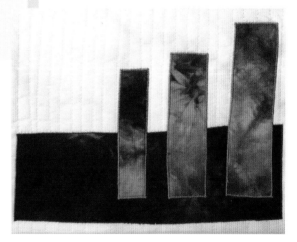

Solid shapes in vertical and horizontal formats appear stationary.

Line is another element used in a unique way by textile artists. Line often comes first with a pencil or paintbrush but is most often stitched near the end of a quilter's construction process. Quilted lines can echo, overlay, or outline the main shapes in a composition. They can take a different direction entirely from the top, adding layers of interest. The gestural quality of a free-motion meandering line can be wide open or microscopically tight and give added texture to negative space.

Because our stitches hold together layers of fabric and batting, they automatically add texture to our composition. If we use a blending color and a lighter weight of thread, our quilted lines seem to disappear. Yet the shadows made by the dips and valleys of the batting add subtle texture. We stitch unbroken lines with our machines or delicate, intermittent lines by hand. If we use a heavy or contrasting color of thread, the element of line moves up the ladder of visual and tactile importance. Lines can also be created by leaving a sliver of space between applied shapes. Lines can be printed on our cloth or added later with an artist's tool such as a brush or pen.

It's important to ask yourself where you want to direct the eye and what effect you want your line to have. Line can be used to suggest the path your eye should follow and where it will rest. Lines can be thick or thin, open or closed, curved, angular, broken, or solid. Frenetic quilted lines that don't quite follow the edge of a shape can evoke anxiety or imply motion. Colorful, spiraling satin stitches can make you feel playful. Solid, heavy outlines can bring calmness and stability to a composition.

Try to anticipate at the beginning of a work how you will quilt your composition. Each element that you add needs to be integrated and well thought out. I often am so caught up in the colors, textures, and shapes of my fabric that I forget

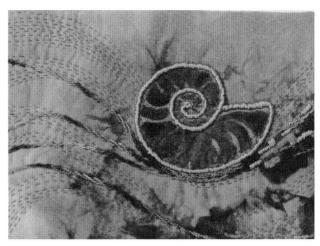

Heavy embroidery as well as delicate running stitches create lines.

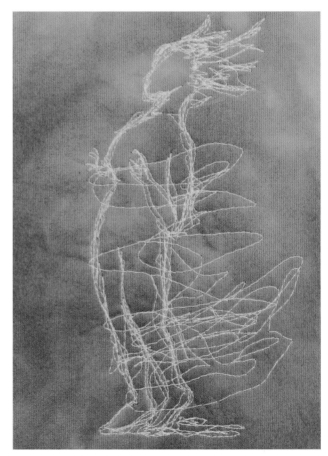

Frenetically stitched lines ecome a sketch in thread.

to think about the quilting until the top is done. It would be easier to have at least a vague plan ahead of time. A good way to test various quilting lines is to take a picture of your work and print it out. Lay a sheet of tracing paper on top of it and use a pencil to test various quilting lines. Vary the weight and direction of the line and see how it affects the composition.

## Gathering Inspiration

Take your sketchbook, window tool, and camera outside or to a new
place and notice the lines all around you. Can you find lines in nature
that are solid and strong or tender and whimsical? Where and how
do they lead your eye? Look through your window tool and find an
interesting composition where line is the dominant element. Quickly
sketch it without worrying about details. Capture the weight of the
line and its direction. Move your window around, looking at more or
less of the scene, thinking about interesting ways to frame the lines you
see. Sketch, then snap some quick pictures for future reference. Try to
capture some different views from those you drew.

# EXERCISE

## Line Weight

1. Make an 8" x 10" (20 x 25 cm) batting sandwich, with a solid fabric on top.
2. Gather many different weights of thread in one color range.
3. Lay out parallel lines of threads and cords.
4. Rearrange them until you're happy with the composition.
5. Vary the weight of the stitched lines to make an interesting composition.

Ask Yourself . . .

*What happens when heavier or lighter lines are placed in different areas?*

*How do different stitch techniques affect the composition?*

*What is the lightest stitched line you can think of? The heaviest?*

6. Use various stitching techniques to create your composition.

## Line as Texture

1. Choose two of the following inspirations (or make up your own): popcorn, nest, trees, stone wall, web, lace, feathers, loops, bricks, spirals, pebbles, stream, echo
2. Using line alone, doodle some ideas with a pencil in your sketchbook.

Ask Yourself . . .

*How heavy or light do your lines need to be?*

*What kind of threads would effectively convey this idea?*

*Can you create this texture with an unbroken, free-motion stitch?*

*Are your lines open and airy, dense and impenetrable, or somewhere in between?*

3. Make two 8" x 10" (20 x 25 cm) batting sandwiches, using a solid fabric on top.
4. Use thread in a color that contrasts with your fabric to interpret your sketch, using stitched lines alone.

Create at least one of your sketched compositions with one continuous line of free-motion quilting.

Lines can be created from the most delicate thread or heaviest bead line.

Textural quilting inspired by the words, "whoosh" and "burst."

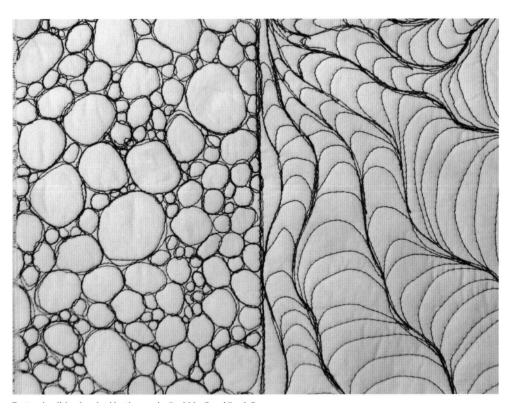

Textural quilting inspired by the words, "pebbles" and "web."

# Free-Motion Machine Quilting

If you can fit a darning foot onto your machine, you can give it a go. Remember that free-motion quilting is another technique that requires practice to perfect. Lots and lots and lots of practice.

With a darning foot in place, drop your feed dogs or set your stitch length to zero. Bring the needle down and back up once to set the stitch; pull the bobbin and top threads to the surface and hold them taut for the first few stitches. Now instead of the machine pulling your fabric as you press the foot pedal, you are responsible for moving the fabric in any direction you choose. Begin moving the fabric slowly but keep the needle moving at a good speed. Slow your hands down (but not the needle) as you change directions. Practice, practice, practice until you are comfortable enough to try it out on artwork you care about.

Further Reading:
*Guide to Machine Quilting*, Diane Gaudynski
*Heirloom Machine Quilting*, Harriet Hargrave
*Quilt Savvy: Gaudynski's Machine Quilting Guidebook*, Diane Gaudynski

Many artists use color in an entirely intuitive way. We know the colors and combinations we like, and we tend to use those combinations repeatedly in our work. We might also have experienced a time when a certain fabric just wouldn't work, and we had no idea why or how to fix it. A basic understanding of the way colors work together can help get us through those frustrating moments.

The first thing we must understand is that color is all about relationships. Not only do we all have a personal and emotional relationship with color, but colors often interact with each other in interesting and unexpected ways. Think of colors as a troupe of actors on a stage. An actress might be an anonymous part of the chorus in one play and the star in the next, just as a red rose might not stand out in a bouquet, but placed in a pile of fish and it becomes the center of attention. Are the colors in your most recent quilt a well-rehearsed ensemble, supporting each other perfectly, helping the star to shine brighter than she could alone, or is a badly behaved color diva stealing the show?

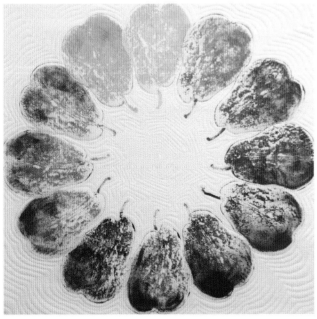

A twelve-step color wheel.

Any three colors that form a triangle on the color wheel are called a triadic color scheme.

Colors next to each other on the wheel are called analogous.

Colors opposite each other on the wheel, such as red and green are called complementary.

## The Color Wheel

Colors in our artwork seldom work alone, just as most theatrical productions need an entire cast of characters. Let's look at a basic twelve-step color wheel and learn how colors relate to each other.

The three colors we begin with are called the primary colors: red, yellow, and blue. They are the main mixing colors, the characters cast first in the play. A printer might use magenta, yellow, and cyan or the dye artist scarlet, lemon yellow, and true blue.

The next three colors on the wheel are the secondary colors: green, orange, and purple. Each is an equal mixture of two primaries.

Oranges, yellows and reds are hot, while greens, blues, and purples are cool.

The six tertiary colors are mixtures of one primary and the secondary next to it, such as yellow-orange, blue-green, and so on. These supporting actors add depth and interest to the play.

When a work of art uses only one color, it is called monochromatic, like a lone actor monologuing on stage. The green involved might vary from a deep forest to a pale lime, but it's still just one spot on the color wheel taking center stage.

When the main colors in a piece are next to each other on the color wheel, the color scheme is called analogous. It could be yellows, oranges, and reds; blues and purples, or any other close combination. The colors are all similar, don't compete for attention, and the resulting artwork is usually calmer than a triadic or complementary color scheme. It is as though the characters on stage are best friends out for a stroll.

When the hero and the villain are duking it out, or Romeo is wooing Juliet at the balcony, the excitement peaks on stage. When colors opposite each other on the color wheel are the dominant players in a work of art, it is called a complementary color scheme. The strong contrast between blue and orange or a warm orange and a cool turquoise creates excitement and sometimes glowing luminosity or subtle vibration.

When the three primaries are on stage at the same time, it is called a triadic color scheme. Each has its own character, attracts a lot of attention, and things are usually pretty lively. Any three colors that form an equilateral triangle on the wheel also form a triadic color scheme when used together as the main colors of an artwork.

Colors also have a temperature: warm or cool. Warm colors usually come from the yellow, orange, and red range and cools come from the blue side of the color wheel. Colors can shift temperatures like an actor playing new roles in each play. A blue can be either warm or cool depending on what it is mixed from and placed next to. Reds can shift toward a cool violet or a warm orange.

Each of these color schemes can be used to your advantage as an artist. Do you want one color to really pop? Place it next to its complement. A vibrant warm orange looks lovely next to yellow, but it will literally jump off the wall if surrounded with deep muddy turquoise. Want a subtler effect? Try an analogous scheme of greens blending into blues with a hint of purple. The relationship the colors have to each other is often more important than the colors themselves.

Our emotional relationships with color can be as individual as our personal list of favorite actors. Colors act on our emotions like players on the stage. Take a good look at your fabric stash and you'll probably find a definite lack of your least favorite color. Do you dislike a certain color? Does it remind you of an unpleasant person, event, or place? Is your stash loaded with bright blue in every pattern imaginable because it's your "happy color"? Take a minute to uncover why you feel the way you do about the colors you love and hate.

An actress can make us laugh in one scene and cry in the next, without ever changing her costume. How does she do it? If she were a color, it would be a simple matter of changing her surroundings. A yellow surrounded by olives and grays might feel sickly and weak. Back it up with a chorus of bright purple and it will dance exuberantly.

Complementary colors of purple and yellow make each other sing.

Consider the emotional way we use color in our language. We "see red," "feel blue," are "green with envy," have a bit of a "yellow streak," or are in a "black mood." Blues used in artwork can evoke the feeling of still tranquil waters, a crisp spring sky, or the grayed shadow of depression. A predominantly blue and green landscape feels calm and serene. The same scene depicted in reds is going to be much more dynamic. Reds are very active and can evoke feelings of passion, danger, or welcome. A child's red ball is joyful, while that same color connotes danger and fear when depicting a pool of blood. Keep in mind that many of these emotional reactions are culturally specific and can vary from place to place. In one part of the world white can signify purity, while in another place it is the color of death. Color is all about relationships with each other, with our emotions, and with our culture.

## Stash Building
### with a color wheel

Time for some fun. Assuming your fabric stash is minimally organized (a big assumption, I know!), sit down with the blank color wheel and fill in amounts for each color you own. Record tints toward the outside and shades toward the inside. See what colors and values you're missing. Do you have a full range of values for each color? No? It's a great excuse for a trip to the quilt shop! Just make sure you have your notes in hand and make a conscious effort to expand your palette.

Look for a blank color wheel online to begin planning your stash.

Further Reading:
*Color Studies*, Edith Anderson Feisner
*The Art of Color*, Johannes Itten
*The Interaction of Color*,
Josef Albers and Nicholas Fox Weber

## Gathering Inspiration

Grab your sketchbook, camera, and something to color with. Try paints, pencils, or the biggest box of crayons you can find. Go outside and observe your environment at different times of the day. As the sky moves from daylight through dusk and into night, notice the color changes and try to capture as many of them as you can. Notice the colors in the sky as you near the horizon. You'll be amazed at how many variations you can find in what used to be a plain blue sky. Watch how the colors of the things around you change as the light changes. If you are lucky enough to catch a sunset, see how many colors you can find and place them on a color wheel.

Carry your sketchbook with you for a week. You never know when something will catch your eye. As you enter each new environment, quickly sketch the color schemes in the décor. Write down how different color schemes affect you and make you feel. Are certain color schemes repeated in the same kinds of places? Look closely at a floral arrangement or the upholstery. Look at a landscape or get right up close to one flower. What color combinations particularly attract your interest? Ask yourself what it is about them that you like. Note any that are surprising to you or that you wish to remember.

# EXERCISE

## Color Relationships

1. Cut four 3" (8 cm) squares from one solid-color fabric.

2. Take the squares to your stash and place them on many different color backgrounds.

3. Use the best lighting you can find (preferably daylight) to view each combination.

4. Look carefully at how different background colors change the perceived color of the squares.

Ask Yourself . . .

*Which two backgrounds change the color of the squares the most?*

*Can you find two different backgrounds that will make the color of the square move from a warm to a cool temperature?*

*What color combination will make the square look exciting, boring, sickly, vibrant?*

5. Cut squares of different backgrounds and create several small color studies, fusing or appliquéing the small squares onto the background squares.

6. If you choose to layer and quilt these studies, use threads that closely match each fabric.

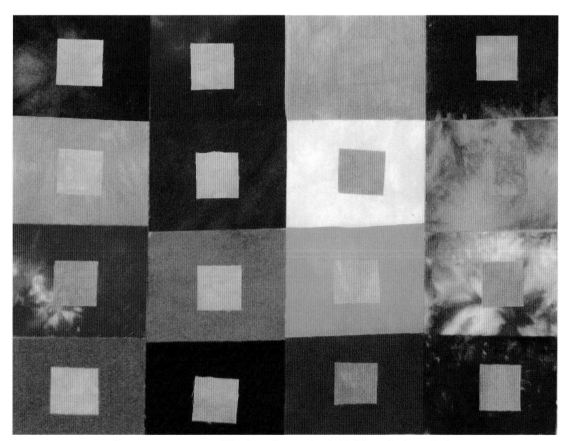

The green squares seem to shift color as they are placed with different background colors.

The same composition in two different color schemes can create either excitement and anticipation or stillness and satisfaction.

## EXERCISE

### Color as Emotion

1. Use an 8" x 10" (20 x 25 cm) piece of batting or muslin as your base.

2. Create a simple composition that evokes a feeling, using color as the dominant element.

3. Choose any emotion as your inspiration, such as the following: fear, courage, apathy, curiosity, calm, energy, hatred, love, sadness, depression, joy.

Ask Yourself . . .

*What color combinations would you use for each emotion?*

*Can you repeat the composition in a different color combination and change the mood?*

4. When you are happy with your composition, fuse or sew it together.

5. Quilt, embroider, or embellish your piece, being mindful of how each new color might add to or change the mood of the piece.

## Value

How dark or light a color appears to be.
A lighter tint or a darker shade of one color.

An actress can have quite a different impact depending if she is in the center of a bright spotlight or lurking in the shadows of the wings. The same thing happens when an object is seen in various light conditions, or when white or black is mixed into a color pigment. The lightness or darkness of a color is called its value. A tint is a color mixed with white, and a shade is mixed with black. When you think of grass you think "green," right? Look at a patch of grass at different times of day and you will see it change drastically depending on how much light is shining on it. At dusk it might even lose its green entirely and become a deep gray blue. Tone is pigment mixed with gray or the color's complement. Think muddy colors.

In art, value is often more critical to the success of the work than color. A turquoise and an orange of the same value placed next to each other will naturally create excitement, but a very dark, low-value turquoise will make a light, high-value orange seem to jump right off of the wall. Many times when a fabric isn't working in a piece, it isn't because it's green, it's because it is the wrong value of green. A lighter or darker green might do the trick. The value of a color will also depend on the value of the colors around it. Take the same medium-blue and place it next to a broad range of yellows. The blue will seem a dark navy on a bright light yellow and will almost glow neon on a deep, dark yellow background.

Different hues have inherently different values as well. Yellows are an inherently light-value color and can only be shaded a little before they aren't considered yellow any more. Blues and purples, on the other hand, are dark to begin with, although they can have a very broad range of values.

In any color scheme, the contrast of values will be like a chorus on stage. They might be dressed the same—a monochromatic color scheme, or they might look different but all be doing the same thing—a low value contrast. Just as highly contrasting complementary colors create excitement, dramatic contrasts in value alone will be very dynamic. The stage will be a very active place if every member of the chorus is doing their own thing. Low-value contrast will result in artwork that is more understated and restrained.

## Gathering Inspiration

This is a time when a digital camera is a valuable tool. If your camera has a black-and-white feature, turn it on and go take pictures of things that capture your interest. Try a close-up picture of mulch or a brick wall. Take pictures of your quilts. Take pictures of a pile of shoes. If your camera doesn't have this feature, you can alter pictures from color to black and white with any basic photo-editing software or make black-and-white prints. See how the values of each picture create an interesting composition. Observe how compositions become more or less interesting without color but with value contrasts.

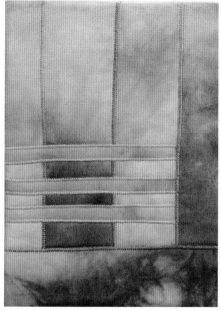
A high-value study.

A low-value study.

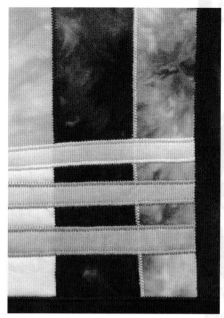
A high-value contrast study, consisting of both light and darks, is the most active and interesting of the three.

# EXERCISE

## Value Contrast

1. Print out several interesting black-and-white pictures. Change the values in the picture by coloring some areas darker and lightening other areas.

2. Fold or tear the paper into smaller sections to focus on areas of interest, creating new compositions. You can also do this with a photocopy of a painting or image from an art book.

Ask Yourself . . .

*How does changing the values change what you see?*

*How do the values attract or move your eye?*

3. Paste your value studies into your sketchbook for future reference.

4. Use three 8" x 10" (20 x 25 cm) pieces of muslin or batting as a base.

5. Sketch out an abstract composition on a piece of paper or use the composition you created.

6. Make three versions of your sketch in fabric using three different value schemes.

7. Make one very high-value contrast, one using only very light values, and one using only very dark values.

Ask Yourself . . .

*How does the mood of each composition alter with a change in values?*

*What words would you use to describe the emotion of each piece?*

8. Gather all the values of one color fabric you can find, from very light to very dark.

9. Create your compositions from these fabrics, seeing how far you can push each one.

10. Use the same color threads and embellishments, in different values, to quilt your piece.

# EXERCISE

## Value and Hue

1. Cut several 2" (5 cm) squares from one medium-value solid fabric. Try to find a pure hue, no tint or shade.

2. Gather all the values of a different contrasting color you can find, from very light to very dark to use as backgrounds.

3. Place the squares on each background.

4. Use the best lighting you can find (preferably daylight) to view each combination.

5. Look carefully at how different background colors change the perceived value of the squares.

Ask Yourself . . .

*Which three backgrounds change the value of the squares the most?*

*What value combination will make the square look exciting, boring, sickly, vibrant?*

6. Cut strips of three different background fabrics and place them on an 8" x 10" (20 x 25 cm) batting.

7. Place the small squares on top of them.

8. If you choose to layer and quilt these studies, use threads that closely match each fabric.

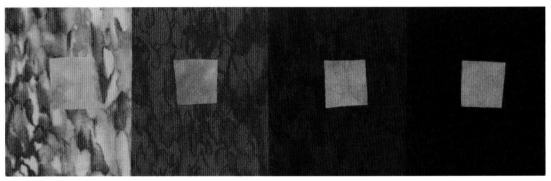

The green appears to shift in value as it is paired with dark to light backgrounds.

Texture, shape, line, color, and value. These are the basic letters in the visual language alphabet. You now know their shape and sound and are ready to move on. Next you'll be learning the principles, the way the letters in this visual alphabet combine to make words in the language of art.

# Using Paint to get Just the Right Color Fabric

Four hundred greens and not a single one is exactly what you are looking for? Not a problem. Find some good-quality textile paints and keep a set of primary colors, plus black and white on hand. If you haven't finished the quilt yet, just mix up the color of paint you need, water it down, and brush it on to change what you've got to what you need. If you've already finished your quilt, go ahead and carefully brush on the paint (practice on a test scrap first) without watering it down. Remember to heat-set the paint according to manufacturer's directions. I've also used oil pastels or colored pencils to alter color or value for art quilts that do not need to be washed.

# CHAPTER THREE

# BUILDING YOUR VOCABULARY:
## The Principles of Design

Once you've worked through the exercises in chapter two, you should have a good grasp of the basic elements, the alphabet used in the visual world. You should be able to recognize and use each element and know the "sound" each letter makes. You're now ready to put the letters together to form words. These principles are the ways in which the elements are put together to make a work of art. Just as with the elements, they overlap in so many ways that it's often difficult to separate and order them. Rhythm is tied to repetition; space and depth are created through the use of proportion and scale, and so on. Let's begin by looking at the principles that make up a work as a whole.

## Unity and Variety
The elements in a work form a pleasing and consistent whole without becoming monotonous.

When you look at a work of art, your mind and eyes process the work as a whole before they begin to notice any separate elements. If all of the elements are working in harmony, you'll see a unified piece where nothing looks out of place. There is a consistent feel to the work; it has a feeling of unity. If you were reading Shakespeare, a single sentence of modern slang thrown randomly into a soliloquy would be jarring and uncomfortable. Its sound is not in harmony with Elizabethan English.

As an artist you are trying to find a consistent style. You want the elements to work together in unity. You could scatter miscellaneous beads, threads, and all sorts of sparkly bits over a gorgeous background fabric, but the separate elements won't create a unified composition unless you are deliberately going for the Jackson Pollock effect. His compositions were unified in their technique, but random in their application. He was more interested in "alphabet soup" than sentences. That's fine, but you need to learn to create meaningful phrases as well. There are three ways to create unity.

The proximity of the letters creates unity in language. When reading the words on a page, you see letters in groupings that convey meaning. Some poets even arrange the words themselves into a pattern that visually reflects the meaning of the words. In artwork, random elements scattered onto a background don't usually read as a visual whole. When you take those same shapes and lines and intentionally place them in proximity to each other, they form relationships that bring harmony to your composition. Your viewer will be able to read them as a unified and interesting whole.

When a group of words repeat a pattern of syllables or sounds, they create a pleasing rhythm. They become poetry or lyrics to music. Unity in artwork can also be achieved through repetition. The blocks and grids of a traditional quilt illustrate the use of repetition as a unifying principle of design. It's possible, however, to have too much of a good thing. Unending repetition won't hold your attention for very long. Variety is needed to keep your interest. The repetition of shape, color, direction of line, or any other element in a work of art can serve to create visual unity while variations in texture or color can give a work more appeal.

Continuation, the third way to achieve unity, is subtler than proximity or repetition. Creating a continuous path of line, shape, or color allows the eye to flow easily from one element to the next. Continuity of technique, texture, or fabric also serves to unify your work. Imagine a traditional Churn Dash quilt in blue cottons with one patch of green silk. No matter how lovely the quilt, that one block is jarring in that context. If you wish to create that effect, go for it. Remember, though, it helps to know the rules in order to effectively break them.

## Gathering Inspiration

Open your favorite art book, and as you look at each picture, find the ways that each artist has created unity. Does the artist use continuity of shape or line as the unifying element? The shapes might overlap and the edges might create a smooth path for your eye to follow. Is unity created through technique, repetition of a color, shape, or direction of line? Have disparate objects been placed in close proximity to create a unified whole? What is the balance between unity and variety? Trace some of the main elements of your favorite artworks into your sketchbook and note what elements were effectively used to create unity. When looking at magazines, observe how graphic designers use continuity as they create a unified look for an entire publication with their use of repeated fonts and layouts.

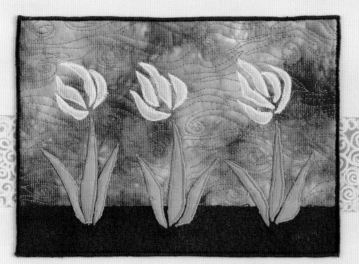

Unity is provided by similar mounting treatments as well as subject matter. Interest comes through variations of color and form. *Windflower Triptych*, each 8" × 10" (20 × 25 cm).

# EXERCISE

## Unity through Proximity

1. Use two 8" x 10" (20 x 25 cm) pieces of muslin or batting as a base.

2. Choose five different fabrics and cut a random shape from each one.

3. Arrange them on your background and try to create unity through proximity.

Ask Yourself . . .

*Is the piece unified or does something look out of place and make you uncomfortable?*

*Will adding or subtracting an element help to create a unified whole?*

*Is there repetition of some element, shape, color, or line?*

*Will adding or removing up to three elements help unify the piece?*

*How can the element of line enhance the unity of this work?*

*Will the addition of embellishments add to or detract from the unity of this work?*

4. Add stitching or embellishments to your work if it will add to the harmony of the piece.

5. Take notes on which exercise you were working on and what you learned.

6. Add this piece (or a picture of it) to your sample notebook.

These shapes are unified only in that they touch each other.

The additional quilting lines and more circles in the same colors as other elements provide unity.

# EXERCISE

## Unity through Repetition

1. Use two 8" x 10" (20 x 25 cm) pieces of fabric and batting as a base.

2. Choose a contrasting piece of fabric and cut out a number of identical shapes.

3. Arrange the shapes in a repeating pattern on your base fabric.

4. Rearrange them several times until you find a pleasing composition.

Ask Yourself . . .

*How much repetition is too much?*

*What would make this composition more interesting?*

*What would happen if you varied one color or shape?*

*How much can you vary each shape and still have a unified composition?*

5. Add the minimum amount of variety to keep a unified whole.

6. Do the exercise again, this time adding the maximum amount of variety without losing unity.

Ask Yourself . . .

*Can you change the color, shape, textures, and sizes without creating disharmony?*

7. Add stitching or embellishments to your work if it will add to the harmony of the piece.

8. Take notes on which exercise you were working on and what you learned.

9. Add this piece (or a picture of it) to your sample notebook.

These repeated shapes vary in only the smallest ways.

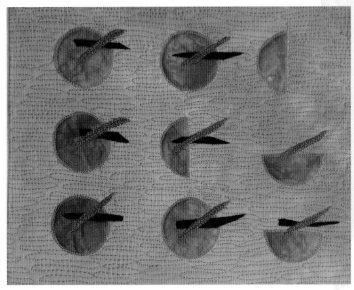

Greater variation in some of the shapes makes a much more interesting composition.

Focal Point
The main emphasis of the work,
the center of interest or activity.

## Choose to *Fuse*

When you're trying to work in a quick and playful way, it can be frustrating to be stymied by technique. Try pre-fusing a selection of fabrics to work with. As soon as you're done creating your composition, just iron it down.

Press your favorite fusible web to the wrong side of a number of fat quarters. Always use a piece of parchment paper or a nonstick pressing sheet to save your iron and board from any unhappy accidents. To avoid frayed edges, peel away the web backing paper before you cut your shapes. It's almost impossible to avoid distorting small shapes if you try to peel the paper off after you've cut out your design. Cutting without the paper will also save your good scissors.

The focal point is the main idea of the piece, the element that first attracts your gaze. It can be the main subject of a narrative piece or simply a point in the artwork where your eye comes to rest. Of course, there are usually other elements that will draw your eye as soon as you have absorbed the main idea. Find an art book and open it to a random picture. As you first glance at a picture, notice what grabs your attention first. Where does your eye go next? Notice the path your eye follows. What is it that draws it there? Artists use a number of techniques to create a focal point in a work of art.

Placement is one of the main ways to create a focal point. The lines and shapes that lead your eye might be as subtle as the gentle curve of an arm or as obvious as a spiraling arrow. Think of a target. The center draws your attention and holds it there. Any element placed in the center of a symmetrical design will also draw your attention like the center of that bull's-eye. Landscapes and architectural scenes will often have many subtle lines leading to one point at the end of a path. Additionally, because we're programmed to follow the implied line of another's gaze,

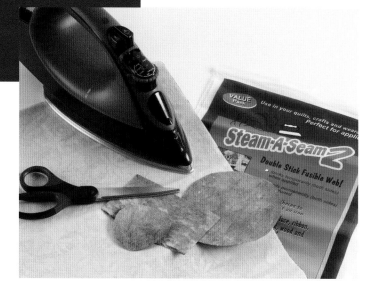

we'll look at whatever someone in a painting is looking at. An element placed in isolation from everything around it will also capture your attention. One block tumbling out of the stack will be noticed, one person standing apart from the crowd always draws your attention.

Any element that contrasts with its surroundings will also attract your attention. A bright red fish in a sea of blue has a strong color contrast. A strong tall vertical element stands out among horizontal elements like a lone tree on the prairie. Textural contrast will attract your eye as well. Open space in the midst of clutter becomes a focal point just as one patterned fabric in a quilt full of solids will naturally attract the eye. Think of a lone realistic image among abstract designs or a large element among many smaller ones. One large bead or one area left unstitched; a contrasting thread, texture, or pattern, each has the potential to become a point of emphasis in any quilt if there is enough contrast.

Of course, you can create lovely works of art without a focal point at all. A traditional quilt can have a harmonious design without any one block catching your eye. Andy Warhol and Jackson Pollock stacked soup cans or scattered drips of paint to create a composition where the eye simply wanders all over the place without ever stopping to rest. Artists can choose which principles to employ just as a poet chooses whether or not to use capitalization, rhyme, or punctuation.

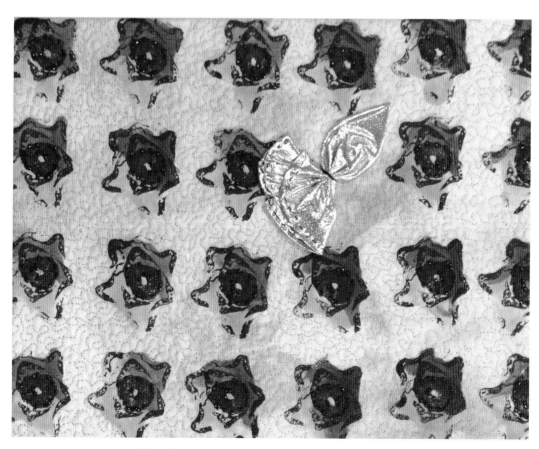

A silver fish in a sea of red roses becomes an automatic focal point.

## Gathering Inspiration

Pay close attention to all of the advertisements you see during your day. What principles and elements have the designers used to capture your interest the first second you glance at the ad? Where is the focal point, and what brought your eye there? It could be the advertised product or something that will evoke a certain emotion. Look at where the text is placed and how it leads the eye as a visual element of line. Block out the main elements of effective ads in your sketchbook and take notes. You don't need to be quite as blatant as an advertisement in your artwork. Simply observing the ads and understanding how a focal point is created will help you better understand and implement this tool.

# EXERCISE

## Focal Point through Placement, Isolation, and Contrast

1. Use three 8" x 10" (20 x 25 cm) pieces of muslin or batting as a base.

2. Choose several shapes to work with and repeat them for each piece.

3. Create three different compositions, using a different tool to create focal points each time:

   1. Use the placement of shapes and lines to lead the eye to a focal point.

   2. Use isolation to create a focal point.

   3. Use contrasts of color, texture, or size to create a focal point.

Ask Yourself . . .

*How could you rearrange the elements to create a stronger path for the eye to follow?*

*Is there a color or value that stands out from the rest of the piece?*

*Does something look different from all the rest? How?*

*How could your stitching and embellishments add to the strength of your focal point?*

4. Add stitching or embellishments to your work if it will add to the strength of the focal point.

5. Take notes on which exercise you were working on and what you learned.

6. Add this piece (or a picture of it) to your sample notebook.

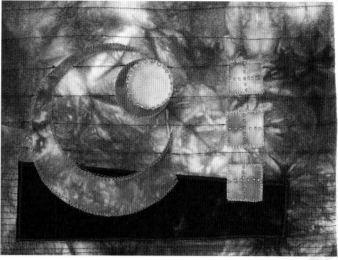

Circles placed within circles become a target-like focal point.

Focal point is created through the isolation of one element and lines that lead the eye.

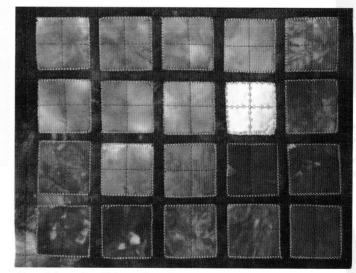

A lone, lighter color will almost always become a focal point.

## Focusing through the lens

As you experiment with different compositions, take a digital picture of each iteration. Sometimes you can't quite remember an arrangement you were happy with after you've moved it, and the digital pictures will help you remember. Seeing a number of pictures together will also help you to quickly see designs that work and those that don't. Try taking or printing out pictures in black and white to test your value contrasts and see if any unintended focal points appear.

Balance is an integral part of our daily lives. We feel stressed when our work and home lives are out of balance. We feel danger when there is imbalance in nature, like a leaning tree or a boulder sitting precariously on a ledge. We quickly try to regain our balance after we stumble, and who can walk by a crooked picture on the wall without reaching out to straighten it? The principle of balance, when executed with skill in a work of art, is almost unnoticeable. When a work is unbalanced, it's uncomfortably obvious.

There are many kinds of balance in the visual world. In a work of art, the largest element or the darkest color usually lies near the lower portion of the frame, lending an appearance of stability and calm. Because we live in a world with gravity, seeing the greatest visual weight near the base feels comfortable to us. Moving the visual weight away from the lower part of the artwork can create imbalance, give the effect of transition, impending motion, or even danger.

Look at much of the architecture around you and you'll find a stately, symmetrical balance, with visual elements mirroring each other around a central vertical axis. In the world of art, symmetry will create a central focal point and can feel quiet and dignified, even static at times. Traditional quilts, such as the Baltimore Album, often make use of symmetrical balance, with motifs arranged around a central medallion. Keep in mind that each element does not need to be an exact copy of its opposite. It is enough to repeat major shapes, lines, and colors to create a symmetrically balanced work.

Crystallographic balance gives equal emphasis to each part of the work, as in most repeated-block patterns. Quilts using this principle, such as the Tumbling Block pattern, usually lack a focal point, which is just fine in this case. Think of a perfectly blended choir where no one voice can be heard above another.

Radial balance is used for Hawaiian appliqué or Mariner's Compass quilts where elements radiate equally in all directions from a central point.

When using asymmetrical balance, each element within the artwork might vary but still receive equal visual weight. A large element in one corner might be balanced by a line leading to an isolated small contrasting element in the other corner. In the visual world, a small area of bright color can balance a larger plain area, just as a complex shape or textured element can balance a larger plain element.

Large empty spaces are balanced by textural interest and a splash of color.

A large simple shape is balanced by a small complex spot of color.

## Gathering Inspiration

Find a book of Asian art or spend some time online searching for images of Japanese paintings or ikebana, a traditional form of flower arranging. You will find a seemingly effortless use of asymmetrical balance. A tiny red bird will offset a heavy mountain; a blossoming branch will lead your eye around the frame without being obtrusive. Notice how a small bit of color will attract your eye and where the lines in the work lead your eye. Observe the intentional use of negative space and that it isn't necessary to fill every bit of your background with images. In your sketchbook, roughly draw the main elements in your favorite pieces and note how the elements are balanced.

As you look at other works of art, ask yourself the following questions: Where is the visual weight of the artwork? Is the artwork balanced symmetrically or asymmetrically? What other elements of art (color, value, texture, shape, line, focal point, scale, unity) are used to create a balanced composition? Keep notes in your sketchbook.

# EXERCISE

## Balance and Color

1. Use an 8" x 10" (20 x 25 cm) piece of muslin or batting as a base.

2. Choose two fabrics, one dull and neutral, the other bright and lively.

3. Cut several shapes from each fabric.

4. Play with the shapes, trying to create a balanced composition.

Ask Yourself . . .

*How much of each color do you need to use?*

*What would happen if you varied the size of the shapes?*

*What would happen if you added one more color to the mix?*

*What would happen if you changed the color values?*

*Can you create a work that is deliberately unbalanced?*

5. Add stitching or embellishments to your work if it will add to the success of the piece.

6. Take notes on which exercise you were working on and what you learned.

7. Add this piece (or a picture of it) to your sample notebook.

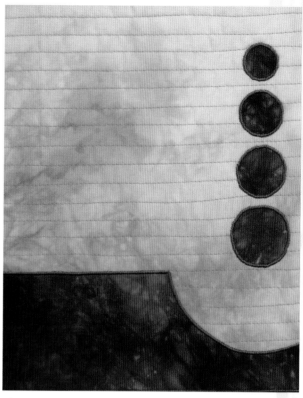

A heavy shape at the lower edge balances and grounds the circles, which seem to float.

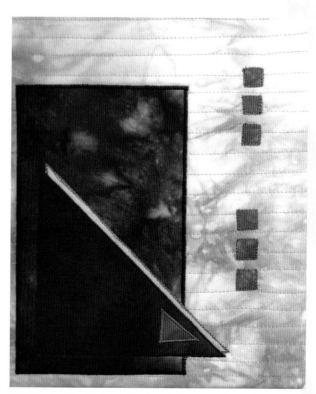

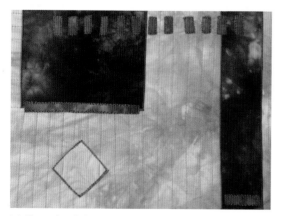

A deliberately unbalanced work, with a heavy weight in the top of the frame feels uncomfortable, even dangerous.

It takes only a tiny bit of a bright color to balance much larger shapes in duller colors.

# Embellishments

We quilt artists love to embellish our work with everything from fuzzy yarns to funky beads and doodads. Each bead, bangle, or layer of burned-out organza will play a role as added color, texture, shape, and line and should be in harmony with the overall composition and must earn its keep. Even tiny beads can alter the balance of your work, can add light and texture, enhance a line, echo an edge, add weight to a shape. A fuzzy yarn might add to a quilt that is already a bit on the wild side, but think hard about whether it will add to the design of the piece.

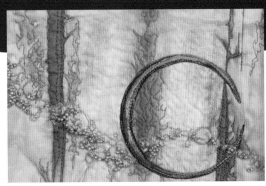

Add embellishments only where they will enhance the design of the composition.

The principle of scale in a work of art is all about the volume of the message you wish to send to your viewer. You could shout out your message to the entire world, or you might wish to whisper into one ear alone. The scale of a work of art in relation to the viewer, its human scale, is often the first consideration an artist makes when working on a commission. Is the artwork going to be displayed on the atrium wall of a large business complex, or will it hang by the front door in a private home? Large-scale quilts are perfect when hung in public spaces and will be able to affect many viewers at once. Private spaces are perfect for small, intricately stitched works and allow for a more intimate experience with the art.

I remember seeing Georges-Pierre Seurat's painting *Sunday Afternoon on The Island of La Grande Jatte* in person for the first time. I'd often seen it pictured in books and enjoyed its pointillist technique. Wandering through the museum's galleries, I rounded a corner and was unexpectedly a foot away from the stunningly large canvas. Its sheer size commanded the attention of everyone in the room, and the impact of the artwork was breathtaking. When your entire field of vision is occupied by a work of art you can't help but to pay attention to it.

Small-scale quilts, on the other hand, will speak to one person at a time, often drawing them physically closer in an intimate exchange of ideas. The impact of the work can be no less enthralling than a large-scale quilt, just as a whisper can have as much meaning as a shout. A tiny beaded and handstitched creation just begs to be touched. Its intimate scale invites the viewer to come close and discover its beauty one stitch and bead at a time.

Scale can also refer to internal proportions, the size of elements within the work itself. The larger the scale of any one element within an artwork, the greater its emphasis. Artists often use exaggerated scale in religious work, drawing a main figure larger than all the others to enhance its importance. Magnifying something that is usually quite small can capture your attention through sheer surprise. A butterfly wing that fills the entire frame gains significance as you see extraordinary details seldom noticed in everyday life. Georgia O'Keefe's enlargements of flowers imbue nature's little wonders with a grandeur seldom seen before her time.

An unnatural contrast of scale in your quilts can also be used to achieve interesting effects. Surrealists such as Salvador Dalí used wildly confused internal proportions to intentionally create uneasiness in the viewer. One element that is purposefully out of scale with other elements within the quilt will attract the viewer's attention and become a focal point.

The same violinist, up close has an entirely different effect on the viewer. *Haven*, 24" × 20" (61 × 51 cm).

The different internal scale of the two figures in this work implies distance. *On Stage*, 10" × 9½" (25 × 24 cm).

## Gathering Inspiration

Stand in front of a mural or go to a museum and stand as close as allowed to a very large-scale work. What is its impact from this distance as opposed to farther back? If you're observing a large public work, take a minute to watch other people's reactions to it. How many passersby turn their heads to look? Find tiny things and draw them at a much larger scale in your sketchbook, noticing details that you have never seen before. Again, don't worry too much about your drawing skills. If your camera has a macro setting, this is a great time to learn how to use it.

# EXERCISE

## Scale

1. Use an 8" x 10" (20 x 25 cm) piece of muslin, fabric, or batting as a base.

2. Go on a treasure hunt and find an interesting object no larger than your thumbnail.

3. Look at the object closely, observing the tiny details.

4. Draw or photograph it. Search the Internet for large pictures of a similar thing.

5. Choose the most interesting part of your drawing or picture and magnify it until it is larger than 8" x 10" (20 x 25 cm).

6. Create a fabric composition from your drawing or photograph.

Ask Yourself . . .

*Is there anything surprising about this tiny thing that you don't normally notice?*

*How does exaggerating the scale of this subject change its importance?*

*Does this subject mean more to you than it did before this exercise?*

*What would happen if you portrayed it in other colors?*

*How do you want a viewer to react to your piece?*

7. Add stitching or embellishments to your work if it will add to the success of the piece.

8. Take notes on which exercise you were working on and what you learned.

9. Add this piece (or a picture of it) to your sample notebook.

The tiny ammonite and the embellishments around it invite you in for a closer look.

The direction of lines within the ammonite blown up to a much larger than life scale form an interesting composition.

## Giving Presence to
## Small Works

Most people don't have much experience with textile art and after seeing a small piece for the first time might wonder why you'd put so much work into a "potholder." Presenting small-scale textile work either mounted or in a frame will tell your viewer that they are seeing art with a capital "A"! Buy a one-inch-thick gallery wrapped canvas larger than your work and paint it or cover it to complement your piece. Then sew your artwork securely to the canvas, checking often to make sure it is straight. This is a wonderful treatment for dimensional works or pieces with irregular edges. A traditional mat and frame, without glass, will also present your work very professionally. If you choose to protect the work with glass, make sure to add spacers so it doesn't touch the cloth.

## Depth and Space
The apparent existence of three dimensions; the empty areas within the frame.

Windows have always held a certain fascination for me. I can gaze for hours at a distant landscape, watch a bustling city scene, or simply watch my children play in the yard. From the outside at night, a lighted window becomes a charming drive-by tableau. Simple rooms become imbued with mystery when viewed through the frame of a window—I'm drawn in and curious.

A window can invite us from one space into another. The space can be expansive or intimate, but it always has depth. It's always someplace we feel we could go to or exist in. In our quilt art, we can invite viewers into our world by using the principles of space and depth, transforming a flat piece of cloth into the illusion of a three-dimensional place. Our minds readily respond to the illusion of depth as though the quilt itself has become a window into the artist's world.

There are a number of techniques quilters can use to create the illusion of depth in space. The simplest tools are size, overlapping elements, and vertical placement. The larger an element is, the closer it appears to be. Simply decreasing the size of a repeated shape will make it appear to be farther away, such as trees marching on their journey down a road. Overlapping elements can also imply depth. Whichever shape is in front appears to be closest to the viewer. Placing an object higher on the plane of the quilt will also imply distance. Look across the room. In order to look at something close by, you must look down at your feet. As your eyes travel into the distance, they lift to the line of the horizon.

When parallel lines in the artwork appear to converge at a vanishing point, perspective is the technique being used to create depth. Choose a point, usually at the horizon line, either inside or outside the borders of the quilt, and draw the lines to meet at that point. If you were to draw lines following the tops and the bottoms of the trees in the sample, they would converge at a point just outside of the upper right corner of the artwork.

How many techniques are used in this piece to imply depth? *Trees*, 5" × 7" (13 × 18 cm).

Color and value are two more tools used to create the illusion of depth. As you look carefully at the landscape around you, notice that far-away objects, such as distant purple mountains, become more blue and gray in color, and the value contrasts, the difference between dark and light, lessen. Objects closer to you will have sharp contrasts in color and value. As you look at *Trees* (page 69), notice that the contrast between the sky and the farthest trees is less than the trees in the foreground. Warm colors such as red and orange also appear to come forward while cool-color objects recede. Volume, the illusion of form, or dimensionality, can also be created with value contrast. If you shade a circle from dark to light, the change in value will visually turn a flat circle into a sphere.

The boundary of your quilt (the border or frame) becomes a window through which your viewer enters your world. If the main subject of a piece is shown in its entirety within a border, it is called closed form. Because you can see the entire work, it seems to be farther away. If you place the subject so that it continues beyond the border, either figuratively or literally, you are using a design principle called open form. The subject appears closer to you either because you can't see the whole thing or because it is coming through the window, or frame of the art.

## Gathering inspiration

Find some landscape photographs or a view of a distance. As you look toward the horizon line, notice what happens to the contrast of colors and the value of those colors. See if you can capture some of those color changes in your sketchbook. What colors do you see in the distance, and how are they different from the colors right at your feet?

Find illustrations of an architectural scene—a picture with buildings in it. Use a piece of tracing paper and trace the horizontal lines in the buildings to a vanishing point. Practice finding the vanishing point in any landscape or architectural scene while looking through a book of your favorite book of artwork.

Depth is implied by overlapping similar shapes in vastly different sizes and in deepening values.

# EXERCISE

## Illusion of Depth through Overlap, Size, Placement, Color, and Value

1. Use an 8" x 10" (20 x 25 cm) piece of muslin or batting as a base.

2. Choose several different fabrics to work with.

3. Cut out one shape in a variety of sizes, ranging from small to large.

4. Overlap the different shapes to achieve the maximum illusion of depth.

5. Place the shapes near the lower portion of your work, then add more, moving toward the top to imply distance.

Ask Yourself . . .

*Which colors and sizes look the farthest away?*

*What happens when you use bright colors in your foreground?*

*What happens if you change the value of the colors in the background?*

*What happens if none of the shapes are overlapping each other?*

*What stitching lines could add to the illusion of depth in this piece?*

*Can embellishments add to the illusion of depth? (Sometimes the answer is no.)*

6. Add stitching or embellishments to your work if it will add to the success of the piece.

7. Take notes on which exercise you were working on and what you learned.

8. Add this piece (or a picture of it) to your sample notebook.

Three flowers are shown almost in their entirety within the frame—closed form.

In open form, the flower exceeds its frame.

## Open Form vs Closed Form

1. Use two 8" x 10" (20 x 25 cm) pieces of muslin or batting as a base.

2. Find or draw a picture of a simple flower or plant.

3. Roughly cut out pieces of fabric to interpret your subject, smaller than 8" x 10" (20 x 25 cm).

4. Create an interesting border to frame the work.

Ask Yourself . . .

*How much depth is there in this composition and can you increase it?*

*Are you drawn in as a viewer?*

*What is the most interesting part of your subject?*

*How can you create an open-form depiction of this subject?*

*Do you think a border will be useful?*

*What would happen if parts of your subject escaped the frame?*

5. Enlarge the most interesting part of your subject so that it fills your 8" x 10" (20 x 25 cm) background.

6. Use your drawing (or tracing) as a pattern to create an open-form composition.

7. Add stitching or embellishments to your work if it will add to the success of the piece.

8. Take notes on which exercise you were working on and what you learned.

## Gaining a Little *Distance*

After working on a piece for a long time, it helps to gain a little distance and view it with fresh eyes. Seeing it from afar will help you catch any glaring compositional, color, or value errors you might not have noticed.

Lay your work on the floor or hang it on the wall and walk as far away as possible before turning to view it. If your space is small, set a mirror on the opposite wall, then stand next to your art and view it in the mirror. This doubles your distance from the artwork and lets you see it in reverse. There are also specialized distance viewing gadgets available, but a less expensive option is the peephole that is installed in a front door. Look through it the wrong way, and it feels like you are very far away from the work. You can also take a digital picture and look at your work on the tiny little screen. Add this piece (or a picture of it) to your sample notebook.

## Motion
The illusion or idea of movement in a work of art.

There is a powerful connection between our visual and our physical selves. When we look at velvet, our fingers know exactly how lush and soft it feels. When we watch a dancer, our own muscles tense as we see her leap and bend. I find it impossible not to move in time to upbeat music. As artists, we can tap into this direct connection between what the viewer sees and feels, by using the principle of motion in our work.

Art that actually is meant to move, such as wearable art or a sculptural mobile, is called kinesthetic art. Creators of "art cloth," defined as the purposeful patterning of cloth as a work of art in and of itself, will often hang their yardage where breezes created by ventilation systems will create literal motion in their pieces. The majority of our two-dimensional artwork however, is meant to hang still on a wall. When we employ techniques that hint at motion in our art, we invite the viewer to become involved, to take part in what they are seeing. There are several techniques that will help imply movement in a work of art.

Horizontal lines and shapes are calm and still, such as a body sleeping, and vertical elements are strong, such as a soldier at attention. When you look at a body in motion, you see many diagonal lines. Think of a runner leaning forward or a dancer arching to the side. Try standing with your own body angled to the ground and you will quickly realize that motion is required to maintain your balance. Angles in nature can also imply motion. Trees with angled trunks remind us of a windswept shoreline. Waves are angled either gently or severely from the ocean's flat surface. Diagonal elements have the most active energy. The eye will slide along a diagonal path more quickly than other directional elements.

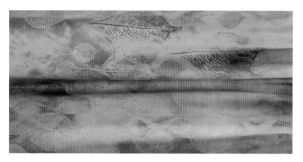

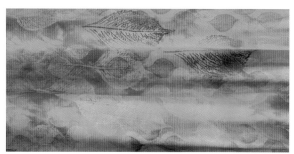

The drapes and folds of art cloth imply motion.

Motion can also be implied through the repetition of a figure in different positions in consecutive frames or overlapping images within one frame. Marcel Duchamp's well-known painting *Nude Descending a Staircase, No. 2* is an example of the cubist's efforts to depict motion as well as form. The figure is painted almost like overlapping time-lapse photographs. Another technique can be borrowed from comic books—it involves adding lines and streaks around a figure that outline the path of motion.

Blurring the outlines of a shape can also imply motion. Quilting stitches that wiggle around and over the edges of a shape, instead of neatly outlining it, can achieve this effect with our usually non-blurrable medium. In fact, next time my machine quilting gets a little out of control I'll just say I was trying to create the illusion of motion in my work! Paint and sheer fabrics can also serve to blur the edges of a shape. You can also blend your colors so subtly that the edges seem to disappear.

A fun illusion of motion easily achieved by an accomplished piecer (or a determined fuser) is called "op art." Abstract geometric shapes and colors are placed in a manner that they appear to actually move or vibrate. Do an online search for "op art" and you will find many interesting examples of planes that appear to move and complementary colors that seem to vibrate.

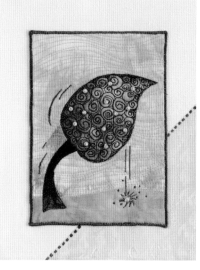

Motion or stillness is created through the angles of shapes as well as through the quilting lines in the background. Borrowed from the cartoon world, little lines imply motion.

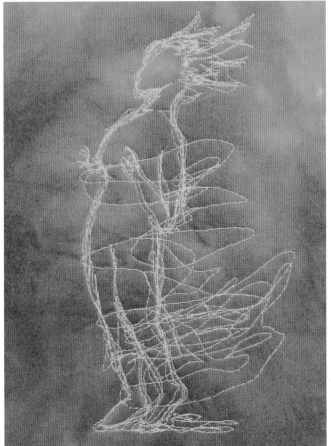

Two compositions, made with line alone, can imply either stillness and calm or frenetic motion.

## Gathering Inspiration

Look around you and think about the angles of shapes and lines and how they are tied to the idea of motion in art. Watch an athlete—the faster they go the more angled their body. Doesn't a curvy Corvette just look faster than a blocky cargo truck? Find a scene of perfect stillness and look at the direction of the shapes and lines. Find a scene of frenzied activity and observe the angles and curves. Open a book of art and notice how many ways different artists can imply motion. Follow the lines of motion with your finger or trace them and place them in your sketchbook.

# EXERCISE

## Line and Motion

1. Make two 8" x 10" (20 x 25 cm) batting sandwiches, with solid-color fabrics on top.

2. Find a picture of a person or animal, preferably standing, showing the whole body.

3. Photocopy or scan it to size it smaller than 8" x 10" (20 x 25 cm).

4. Trace the outlines of the figure without worrying about details.

5. Transfer these outlines to your fabric with a pencil. (Tape it to the window or use a light table.)

6. Using contrasting thread, drop the feed dogs on your machine, use a darning foot, and free-motion quilt the figure outline. Don't worry about being careful or exact. Go over the stitches in a wiggly and quick way. Perhaps even add squiggles, loops, or dashes where motion might occur.

7. Try to create as much motion and frenzy as you can with line alone.

Ask Yourself . . .

*Where do you see the most motion in your creation? What kind of background would add even more motion to this exercise?*

8. For the second quilt sandwich, try to create as much stability and calm with line as you can.

   – Try a smooth satin stitch to outline the figure.

   – Add any other lines you think might help with a feeling of stillness and stability.

9. Take notes on which exercise you were working on and what you learned.

10. Add this piece (or a picture of it) to your sample notebook.

The angled body of this runner implies impending motion.

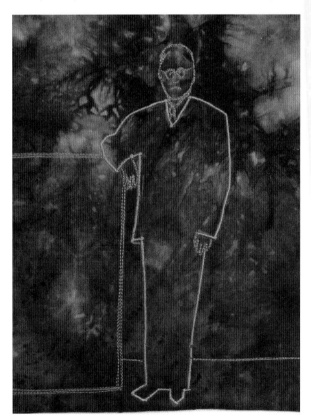

Predominately vertical and horizontal lines imply stillness.

# EXERCISE

## Motion through Line Direction

1. Use two 8" x 10" (20 x 25 cm) pieces of fabric or batting as bases.

2. Cut a number of similar squares from one piece of fabric.

3. Arrange them on your background, trying to create as much motion as you can.

Ask Yourself . . .

*What angles create the most movement?*

*What happens when you vary the size of the squares?*

*What would happen if you cut several, or all of the squares into triangles?*

*Do you think motion would be easier to imply with rounded shapes?*

4. Create a second composition with the same squares, this time aiming for a feeling of calm and stillness.

Ask Yourself . . .

*What angles create the most movement?*

*What happens when you vary the size of the squares?*

*What stitched lines would add to the tranquility of this piece?*

5. Add stitching or embellishments to your work only if it will add to the success of the piece.

6. Take notes on which exercise you were working on and what you learned.

7. Add this piece (or a picture of it) to your sample notebook.

The angles of these shapes and the variation in size create motion.

# Finishing Small *Textile Pieces*

You can use a traditional binding, but for small pieces, I choose a quicker and easier method, especially good for irregularly shaped edges. Lay a pre-fused piece of fabric face down on the front of your piece. Sew all the way around the edges without leaving a gap. If you stretch the fused fabric a bit as you sew, it will pull to the back after you turn it so that it won't show at the edges.

Trim the seam allowances and the corners. Carefully pinch the fused backing up from the top and cut a diagonal slit large enough to turn the piece right side out. Be careful not to cut your artwork.

Turn the piece right side out and carefully prick and poke out the corners and smooth the seams with your fingernails. Use a hot iron and carefully press, from the back, starting in the corners and working toward the slit. Take your time, working with the piece as you fuse it to keep it in shape. Once the slit has been closed, fuse a label right over the top of it.

ONE NATION
In honor of September 11, 2001
by LYRIC M. KINARD
Cary, North Carolina

We are
ONE NATION
No matter where we came from
UNDER GOD
No matter what name we give Him
With
LIBERTY
And
JUSTICE
For
ALL

None should fear for the sake of
race or religion
We must stand
UNITED
Without
FEAR

If we are to prevail
WE WILL RISE UNITED!

Rhythm is a unifying principle in art as well as our lives. Our hearts beat in rhythm, and even the seasons pass in patterns. In music and dance, rhythms measure and divide time and space. Visual rhythm involves the movement of our eye from one element to the next in a regular pattern. There are as many kinds of visual rhythms as there are musical rhythms. We've learned that repeated elements will help bring unity to our artistic creations, but it is the rhythm—the pace and pattern of those repetitions—that will help us convey movement on the still, flat plane of our artwork.

A regular rhythm is like the steady beat of our heart or the gait of our walk. Think of the repeated vertical stripes of a strong and simple Amish bar quilt or the rising diagonal lines of a Log Cabin block set in a straight furrows variation. The curving, repeated elements of a Fan block set in diagonal stripes are restful, soft, and carry our eye in the same way legato notes flow smoothly together. In a staccato visual rhythm, the eye must jump instead of flow from one element to the next, such as with a repeated Carolina Lily block marching across a plain background, each motif standing alone yet in harmony with its mates.

Alternating rhythm is the variation of a repeated pattern between two or more elements, such as the pattern of night and day or a chorus repeated between different verses of a song. A syncopated rhythm gives surprising emphasis to a beat that is normally weak and adds unexpected interest, just as interspersing a pattern of large and small elements in a surprising pattern will add movement and excitement to a work of art.

A progressive rhythm is often found in nature when the size or shape of something gradually increases or decreases. Picture the growing concentric layers of tree rings or the regular pattern of a rose's opening petals. Think of a musical theme that grows in complexity, volume, and instrumentation with each repetition, or look at the gradually diminishing pattern of ocean waves as your eye moves toward the horizon. In visual art, a progressive rhythm might consist of any repeated element growing or shrinking in size, shape, or number. The expanding rays of a Mariner's Compass block as it reaches outward are a great example of progressive rhythm.

Gentle horizontal waves that progressively recede into the background create a smooth legato rhythm.

Separate repeating elements create a regular staccato rhythm.

## Gathering Inspiration

Grab your sketchbook and camera and go find some rhythm! See how many kinds of rhythms you can find. Look for the progressive shortening of branches as you climb the trunk of a pine tree, the alternating rhythm of light spaces and dark trees in a forest, or the regular pattern of lines in a parking lot, or the windows of a structure. Office buildings are particularly interesting at night with their irregular patterns of light and dark windows. Allegro means fast and bright while adagio means slow and stately. Each of these rhythms presents a different feeling to the viewer—serenity, activity, excitement, or haste. Can you find and sketch visual representations of these tempos?

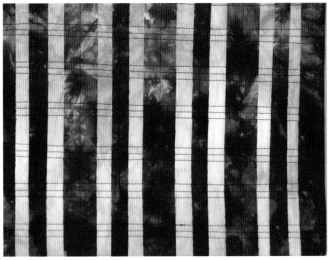

Symmetrically placed strips create a regular rhythm.

## EXERCISE

## Rhythm through Repetition

1. Make an 8" x 10" (20 x 25 cm) batting sandwich, with solid-color fabric or muslin on top.

2. Using a solid contrasting color, or black fabric, cut at least four strips of each width, from ½" to 2" (1.3 to 5 cm).

3. Arrange them in regular patterns on your background to create a rhythmic pattern.

Ask Yourself . . .

*What is the feel of the rhythm you've created?*

*Would it feel different if you rotated your composition 90 degrees?*

*What if you thought of your background as your foreground?*

*How many different rhythms do you think you could create in this manner?*

*How could stitching or embellishments further enhance the rhythm of this piece?*

4. Stitch or embellish this work if it will strengthen the rhythm you've created.

5. Take notes on which exercise you were working on and what you learned.

6. Add this piece (or a picture of it) to your sample notebook.

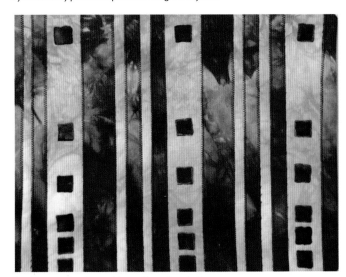

Breaking up a few lines adds an alternating rhythm.

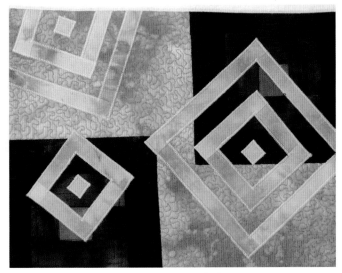

The change of square sizes creates a progressive rhythm.

# Meditatively Modify
## your meander

Free-motion quilting can be very rhythmic and meditative once you get the hang of it. If you are tired of the ubiquitous stipple meander or wish to try quilting without marking first, try this: Simply take pencil and paper in hand and start doodling without ever lifting the pencil. Once you find a design you'd like to try, repeat it several times. As your hand moves and your eye follows, it will give you a head start for trying it out with your machine.

Further Reading:
*72 Ways Not to Stipple or Meander,*
Dijanne Ceval (self-published, visit http://origidij.blogspot.com)
*Mindful Meandering,*
Laura Lee Fritz

The elements of art are the letters of the visual alphabet, the principles are the combinations that form words: unity and variety, focal point, balance and symmetry, scale and proportion, depth and space, motion and rhythm. Are you ready to gather your words into meaningful phrases, to create that magic world of the imagination that comes from the mind of an artist? I know you can do it! Let's move on to some design exercises that will help you to begin your narrative in the visual language.

# CHAPTER FOUR

# WRITE ON:
## Creative Composition

Now what? Shakespeare didn't write *Romeo and Juliet* when he was six years old! It's most likely that he began just like the rest of us, by writing a lot of awkward verses and rambling essays. He practiced until he developed the skills necessary to become one of the greatest writers in English history. If you have the fire in your heart to become an artist, you need to do your homework. You need to practice a new way of thinking. If you can't bring yourself to say it aloud, I challenge you to spend a few minutes each day "pretending" you are an artist. Imagine it long enough, practice it willingly enough, and it will come true. It's amazing to me how often children live up to our expectations. Set your expectations high for yourself!

## Homework Assignments and Field Trips

Wouldn't it be lovely if you could find forty-five minutes every day for your art? Turn off the TV for an hour. Take a fifteen-minute break during lunch or after work, to imagine and be inspired. Wake up thirty minutes early or stay up half an hour later to play with some art and experiment. Give yourself the wonderful gift of filling your well with inspiration. Once a month take yourself, and perhaps a collaborator, to anywhere that interests you and seek inspiration.

### 5 minutes to imagine

Find a quiet place, shove the laundry list out of your mind, and spend a few minutes with your eyes closed. Daydream. Begin with your wishful desires, think of your goals, and let your creative mind wander. Write your dreams in a sketchbook or journal without fear or self-criticism! You need never show or tell these thoughts to anyone unless you wish to.

### 10 minutes for inspiration

Look around with your new artist eyes and choose a basic design element or principle to look for. Look at the products in your kitchen. Take a short walk. Turn the pages of an art book; notice how each artist or designer has used that tool. Sketch the basic idea and write down what you've learned.

### 30 minutes to make art

As you begin to use the visual language it will take some practice to become fluent. Give yourself permission to experiment without expecting perfection. Stick with an 8" × 10" size project, set the timer, and forge ahead without fear. Choose a design game from the next few pages and work for thirty minutes. Venture beyond your comfort zone and try something new. Play. Fail. Learn. Succeed. Most of all HAVE FUN!

### Field trips

Set a date; bring your sketchbook, camera, and perhaps a friend. Go to a museum, park, gallery, grocery store, downtown, or anywhere interesting, and contemplate your surroundings with an artist's eyes. Be inspired. Look for exquisite compositions, well-balanced forms, and distinctive color combinations. Be inspired by a beautiful flower and the flotsam in the gutter. Sketch it, write about it, photograph it. Write down what inspires you and why. When people see your sketchbook and come to look, tell them, "I am an artist!"

## Playing the Design Game

Copy each page and cut out the Elements and Principles cards on pages 88–89.

Randomly choose one element card or one principle card and create an 8" x 10" composition concentrating on that one thing. Choose the variation of the element or principle that interests you or one that is a challenge. Once you have worked through each of them, combine an element with a principle.

Work as quickly as you can for thirty minutes. Remember to play, fail, learn, succeed, and grow—and most importantly, HAVE FUN! Any of these exercises are easily adapted to group work. Encourage each other to let loose and play. Get together at the end of your play session and run through the critique questions in Chapter 5. Eat lots of chocolate!

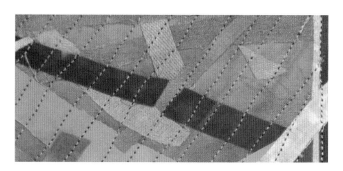

## Rephrase, Please
Express an idea in an alternate way.

Choose an element card and do something interesting to it. Choose one of the actions below:

- Add, Subtract
- Bend, Straighten
- Bridge, Partition
- Clarify, Confuse
- Divide, Multiply
- Exaggerate, Minimize
- Fracture, Weave
- Flatten, Texturize
- Hide, Feature
- Layer, Separate
- Nestle, Isolate
- Pierce, Mend
- Randomize, Grid
- Sharpen, Soften
- Stretch, Squash

## Nouns
Noun, being the element about which the rest of the clause is predicated.

Pick an element card, then concentrate on one of the subjects below. If you're feeling ambitious, work with a principle card as well. You don't need to interpret your subject literally. Concentrate more on the idea of the thing and how you can represent it with your chosen element and/or principles.

Subjects
- Tree, Vegetable, Fruit, Flower, Garden, Landscape, Prairie, Swamp
- Woman, Child, Man, Family, Boy, Girl, Alien, Outsider
- Cat, Frog, Fish, Elephant, Bird, Dog, Lizard, Monster, Zebra, Gazelle
- Spring, Summer, Autumn, Winter, Heat, Ice, Breeze, Hurricane
- Home, Retreat, Office, Escape, Cocoon, Prison, Cafe
- Web, Lace, Stone, Water, Cloud, Pebble, Stream, Mountain, Feather, Nest

## Searching for a Muse
The place in which an artist finds the inspiration for a creative endeavor.

Pick an element and go on a treasure hunt. Find an example of that element and bring it back with you, take a picture, or draw a sketch of it. Draw a random principle and work like a fiend for thirty minutes, using your treasure as an inspiration.

Variations with a group or on your own:

- Find several interesting objects and place them on a table. Everyone works with the same inspirations but chooses different elements to work with.

- Choose one element for everyone to work with and spend ten minutes hunting for individual inspirations. Everyone chooses a different principle to work with.

- Choose different elements and have everyone find an actual object. Place all the group's objects on a table, labeling each with its element card. Randomly distribute the items before drawing principle cards.

## Poetic License

Special intensity is given to the expression of feelings and ideas by the use of distinctive style and rhythm.

Find a book of poetry and open it to a random spot. Choose either an entire poem or a few random words and use these as a springboard for your creation.

Variations:

- Have a group or partners interpret the same words.

- Give each person a different element to concentrate on.

- Interpret the text three times, each time with a different element.

- Have each person contribute one word to a new poem for the group to interpret.

- Choose one poem for the group, have each person interpret a different stanza, concentrating on a different element and principle.

## Music to the Eye

The art or science of combining sounds to produce beauty of form, harmony, and expression of form, harmony, and emotion.

Choose your favorite piece of music. Pachelbell's Cannon in D is an excellent piece to begin with. Close your eyes and listen

intently to the rhythm of each new motif. Listen again with your sketchbook in hand and freely doodle as many sketches as you can while the music lasts. Choose a likely idea from your doodles and interpret your music visually. Look through your sketches and choose the one that most closely resembles your visual interpretation of the music and create it in cloth.

Variations:

- Listen with an element card in hand, imagining what that element looks like dancing in rhythm to the music.

- Interpret someone else's favorite piece of music.

- Interpret the same piece multiple times, concentrating on a different element each time.

- Choose one dominant color for the group to work with and have each person find a piece of music from their collection to interpret.

## Collaborative Collage

A jointly worked composition.

By yourself, pick three elements to concentrate on. Work for ten minutes on the first element, ten minutes on the next, and ten minutes on the third.

With two or three collaborators, each of you work on the same element for the first ten minutes, then the second element for the next ten minutes, etc.

Variations:

- Work on your composition for ten minutes, then trade with a partner for the next ten minutes. Trade back or with a third collaborator for the last ten minutes, each of you working on the same element.

- Choose three different element cards and add one principle card. Begin with your first element card and a principle. After ten minutes switch to your second element, still working with the same principle. The last ten minutes switch to your third element, still concentrating on the same principle.

- With a group, do the above exercise, trading pieces every ten minutes, working on the same three elements, but each collaborator concentrates on a different principle.

ELEMENTS
## texture

- The way something feels to the touch or the visual patterns on a surface.

- Bold, Subtle, Rough, Smooth, Feathery, Sharp, Tactile, Actual, Imitation

ELEMENTS
## line

- A mark, long in proportion to its breadth, made on a surface with a pen, pencil, tool, etc.

- Parallel, Angular, Curved, Broken, Solid, Directional, Gestural, Heavy, Light, Frenetic, Controlled, Textural

ELEMENTS
## value

- How dark or light a color appears to be. A lighter tint or a darker shade of one color.

- High Value, Low Value, Medium Value, High Contrast, Low Contrast

ELEMENTS
## shape

- A closed two- or three-dimensional form encased by a line or an edge. A distinct visual unit.

- Active, Stationary, Rounded, Angular, Solid, Complex, Simple, Abstract

ELEMENTS
## color

- The hue of an object or its name: green, blue, etc.

- Monochromatic, Analogous, Complementary, Triadic, Cool, Warm

PRINCIPLES
## unity and variety

- The elements in a work form a pleasing and consistent whole, without becoming monotonous.

- Proximity, Rhythm, Pattern, Continuation, Color

# focal point

- The main emphasis of the work, the center of interest or activity.

- Placement, Contrast, Isolation, Scale, Color

# rhythm

- The repetition of a regular pattern or a harmonious sequence or correlation of colors or elements.

- Staccato, Legato, Regular, Alternating, Progressive

# motion

- The illusion or idea of movement in a work of art.

- Implied, Angular, Quiet, Languid, Frenetic, Blurring, Overlapping

# balance and symmetry

- The distribution of visual weight in a work of art, the harmony of design and proportion.

- Asymmetrical, Symmetrical, Radial, Crystallographic, Unbalanced

# space and depth

- The apparent existence of three dimensions/the empty areas within the frame.

- Overlap, Size, Color, Value, Placement, Perspective, Open Form, Closed Form

# scale and proportion

- The size of a work in relation to humans; the size of elements within the work in relation to each other.

- Exaggerated, Intimate, Grand, Magnified

# Student Gallery

Many thanks to the brave volunteers who agreed to try out these exercises and share their results with you. As you can see, some are the raw exercise, completed when the timer went off. Other students went on to stitch and finish their work. Let me remind you again, this is a learning process. Have fun with it. Drop your expectations of perfection and simply absorb each concept as you explore it.

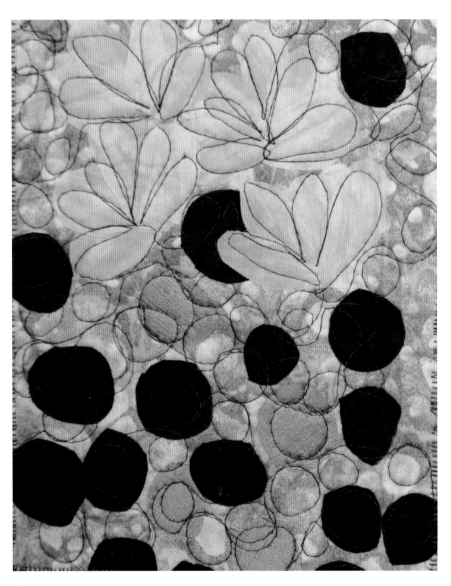

Element: Value
Principle: Focal point/Contrast
by Ann Flaherty

Element: Color/Hot
Principle: Rhythm/Legato
by Eileen Klee Sweeney

Element: Line
Principle: Motion
by Eileen Klee Sweeney

Principle: Rhythm
Subject: Landscape
by Eileen Klee Sweeney

Principle: Rhythm
Element: Texture
by Judith Glover

Principle: Scale
Subject: Autumn
by Ann Flaherty

Element: Texture
Principle: Motion
by Judith Glover

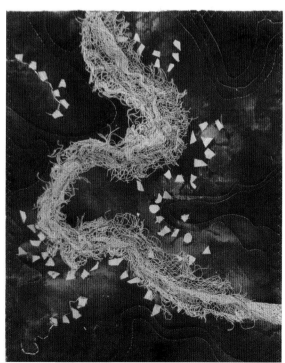

Elements: Shape and Color/Complementary Principle: Rhythm/ Repetition
by Kathy Hefner

Element: Color Principle: Unity Subject: Forest
by Patty VanHuis-Cox

Element: Line
Variation: Fractured
Principle: Focal point

by Mary Jo Bowers

Element: Color and Value
Principle: Rhythm

by Rita Legere

Element: Color/Complementary
Principle: Depth/Placement

by Rita Legere

Elements: Shape and
Color/Triadic color scheme

by Rita Legere

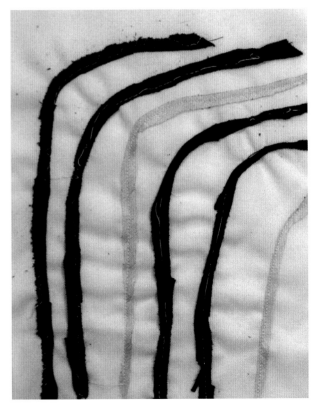

Element: Line
Variation: Bend
Principle: Motion

by Rita Legere

Element: Color
Principle: Balance/Asymmetrical
Subject: Flower

by Kathy Hefner

Principle: Motion/Rhythm/Legato
Subject: Stream
by Roxane Lessa

Element: Shape/Rounded
Principle: Scale
by Mary Jo Bowers

Element: Shape
Variation: Active
by Mary Corcoran

Element:
Color/Complementary
Principle: Balance/
Symmetrical
by Karen Fridy

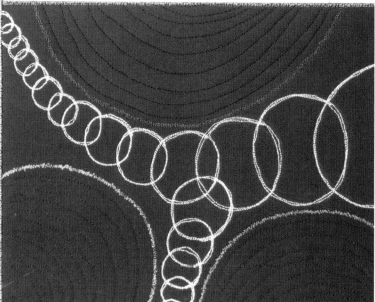

Elements: Line and Texture
Principle: Unity
by Karen Fridy

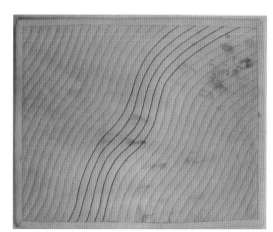

Element: Line
Principle: Focal point
by Dale Anne Potter

Element: Shape
Principle: Motion
by Diane Petersmarck

Element: Color
Principle: Symmetry
Subject: Tree
by Dale Anne Potter

Principle: Space
Subject: Woman

by Amy Eileen Koester

Element: Shape
Principle: Motion

by Stephanie Nordlin

# CHAPTER FIVE

# POETRY:
# The Art of Evaluation and Critique

*"The trouble with most of us is that we would rather be ruined by praise than saved by criticism."*

—*Norman Vincent Peale*

Receiving constructive feedback on your artwork can be incredibly valuable. It's common to be so close to your work that you simply don't see it clearly anymore. The details may consume your attention, and you forget to look at the big picture. Going through the questions in this chapter will help you see your own work with a fresh and critical eye. It can be even more helpful to find a group of friends you can trust to give you honest and kind opinions.

Remember the multiple-choice tests you took in school? Every question had one right answer and all the rest were wrong. Not so for an essay. You might think you are writing beautifully, making a clear point, and then your professor gives it a terrible grade.

I remember one professor I dreaded. The essays would come back with big red letter grades, sometimes good, sometimes not. Nothing else, no feedback. There was another professor I adored. Essays would come back with notes scribbled all over them, suggestions for improvement, every little grammar error marked, but the occasional compliment as well. The grades achieved in both classes were similar, but I feel I learned a great deal more from the professor who gave me feedback. He helped me improve. Even if something stank, he'd say why, then cushion my bad grade with the comment, "I know you can do better."

Just remember that art is like that essay test back in school. Every observer of your work will have a different opinion about it. Each of us wears a different pair of glasses, crafted by our unique experiences, through which we interpret the visual world. Follow the guidelines outlined below and listen carefully to the evaluations. Separate yourself from the work and give yourself time to absorb the analysis. You may choose to accept or reject the opinions and recommendations of your friends.

The important thing to remember is that a good critique can help you improve the quality of your work. Look at every single piece of work as a learning process and REALLY look for what you need to do to improve. Listen. Absorb. Learn.

## Uninvited Criticism

"Don't mind criticism. If it is untrue, disregard it. If it is unfair, keep from irritation. It if is ignorant, smile. If it is justified, learn from it." —*Anonymous*

Learning to deal with rejection and criticism comes right along with your growing self-confidence as an artist. You must learn to divorce your personal self-worth from the finished product and accept that everyone has very different tastes. No one has ever created something that everyone loves, and every piece you make will not be a masterpiece. Just because someone doesn't like something you've produced doesn't mean that they don't like you. If you happen to overhear an unkind remark, let it go. It can only hurt you if you choose to believe it.

If you are your own worst critic, finding fault with every miniscule imperfection, ask yourself who it is you are listening to. Is your artwork telling you what it needs? Are quilt police counting stitches or is your home economics teacher being unfairly nitpicky? If it's the work, trust it. If it's not, don't let one microscopic imperfection ruin your enjoyment of a lovely piece.

Remember to be kind and generous with your praise. You never know who's listening, and a picky comment at a quilt show could devastate a fragile ego. Unless you've been invited to formally critique a work, stick to the "if you can't say anything nice, don't say anything at all" rule.

# The Rules of the Game on Your Own

"One should never criticize his own work except in a fresh and hopeful mood. The self-criticism of a tired mind is suicide."

—*Charles Horton Cooley*

If you're working alone, give yourself as much distance as possible. Leave your work alone for a few days, if possible without looking at it, then bring it out for a critique. Start by placing the work as far away from you as possible. (See the sidebar in Chapter 3, page 73, "Gaining a Little Distance.")

Try your best to be objective as you go through the list of questions in this chapter. Begin by asking yourself what it is you wish to learn. Are you seeking a better understanding of design principles, or are you trying to communicate a clear message? Are you working on a technical skill or trying to strengthen an area in which you are weak?

# The Rules of the Game With a Group

"Criticism, like rain, should be gentle enough to nourish a man's growth without destroying his roots." —*Frank A. Clark*

A good critique is an invaluable tool, but group critiques can be fraught with difficulties. Emotions and egos can get involved, and feelings can be hurt. A well-run critique can help you grow by leaps and bounds if you allow yourself to be open to the learning process. Again, ask yourself what it is you wish to learn from the group. Think through this question before you show your work, and make sure your friends know what you're looking for. Perhaps you simply want support and encouragement and wish to share what you've learned in the process of making the work. And remember, it is always you, the artist, who will make the ultimate decisions about the work.

## Set Up

- Give each artist/work equal time, at least fifteen minutes. Use a timer so you don't run out of time.
- Display each work on the wall if possible, making sure it's well-lit. A large piece of foam board works well as a portable design wall.

## Describe

- The artist describes the facts about the work.
- The artist also tells the group what it is he/she wants from a critique of this work.

## Analyze and Interpret

- While the artist is silent, every person takes an equal amount of time to comment.
- Don't let one person dominate the conversation.
- Observe and analyze, don't judge.
- Say, "I see ____" rather than, "I don't like ____."
- Option: Have each person write down the first three words they think of when they see the art, then talk about that.

## Question

- The artist answers questions and begins to absorb what other people are seeing.
- Ask leading questions to help the artist find his/her own solutions.
- Don't point out problems without providing possible solutions.

## Judge

- Answer the questions from this section only if the artist wishes.
- Think of what the artist might want to hear, not what YOU would like to hear.

## Review

- Have a different person summarize each review so that all feedback doesn't seem to come from one person.

**Critique**

*A detailed definition or assessment. An appraisal or study with commentary and feedback.*

Carefully go through each relevant question. Be thoughtful and helpful yet as truthful and objective as you can.

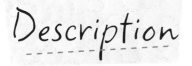

**Description**

*To give an account, including all the relevant characteristics and qualities.*

---→ *How is the piece displayed?*

Objective Facts of the Work

- Artist, date, size, title.
- Is the work in progress or finished?
- Is the piece part of a series?
- What is the subject matter?
  *Landscape, figure, still life, non-objective, other*
- What is the style of the piece?
  *Abstract, complex, decorative, folk, functional, impressionistic, non-objective, minimalist, outsider, op-art, realistic, representative, Rococo, simplistic, surreal, symbolic, sculptural*

*Untitled Small Work,* 5" × 7" (13 × 18 cm)

--→ *Describe the materials and techniques used to create this piece.*

*Three Leaves*, 13" × 10" (33 × 25 cm)

## Materials Used in the Work

- Fiber/fabric

  *Cotton, silk, burlap, velvet, corduroy, wool, paper, tissue, synthetic, metallic*

- Patterning

  *Solid, plain, print, striped, plaid, conversation print, batik, hand-dyed, striped*

- Weave

  *Plain woven, brocade/satin, twill, open weave, novelty*

- Embellishments

  *Thread, cord, yarn, beads, etc.*

## Techniques Used to Create the Piece

*Piecing, appliqué, whole cloth, dyeing, painting, shibori, discharging, printing, novelty (yo-yos, folding), fusing*

*Machine quilting, handquilting, embroidery, seed stitching*

*Computer printing, photo transfer, lettering, stenciling, stamping*

## How is the Piece Displayed?

*Hanging, mounting, framing, standing alone*

# Analysis

*A detailed examination of the elements or structure of the work.*

Looking at the work objectively, answer the following:

---

---> *What is the relationship between the elements in this work?*

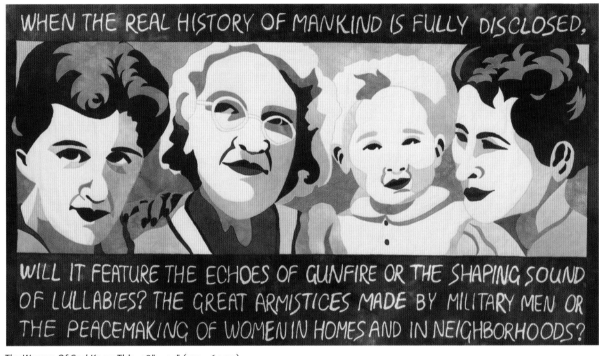

*The Women Of God Know This*, 48" × 25" (121 × 64 cm)

Overall Structure of the Work

- How is the work organized?
- What is the structure of elements?
- What is the relationship between the elements?
- How are the design principles used?
- What is this work similar to?
- What elements within the work are similar?
- What elements within the work are different?
- Does the art have a message?

---> *Describe the actual texture of the work.*

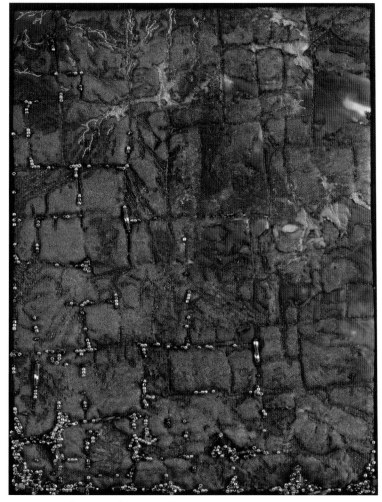

*Rust,* 8" × 10" (20 × 25 cm)

## Use of texture

- Which texture catches your eye first, and why?
- What is the actual (tactile) texture of the work?
- What technical challenges does this material present?
- How does the texture of each cloth affect the outcome of the piece?
- What is the visual texture of the work?
- Does any one pattern in the fabric stand out? Should it?
- Is depth, motion, or a focal point created through the use of a visually patterned cloth?
- Is the visual texture imitating an actual texture?

*---→ How does the negative space affect the positive space?*

*Place*, 22" × 18" (56 × 46 cm)

## Use of Shape

- What are the major shapes of the piece and how do they lead the eye?
- Are the shapes integrated into the background, or do they float in space?
- How does the negative space (background) affect the positive space (foreground)?
- Which shapes appear to be dominant in this piece?
- Do the shapes create a feeling of stillness or of activity? How?
- Are the shapes representative or abstract?

## Use of Line

- What is the dominant direction of line, and where does this lead the eye?
- What is the weight of line in this piece?
- What emotions are evoked with line in this piece?
- How dominant are the quilting lines in the composition?
- Do the quilted lines accentuate or counter the main shapes in the work?
- Do the lines in this piece act primarily as texture?

*Stone, Water, Time,* 20" × 42" (51 × 107 cm)

*--→ Is there high or low contrast in the values used?*

*Mother's Hand: Burnt Out,* 16" × 22" (41 × 56 cm)

## Color and Value

- What color schemes are used?
  *Triadic, monochromatic, complementary, analogous*
- Is there one color that stands out or a dark or light spot that draws the eye?
- Is there high or low contrast in the values used?
- How does the value contrast affect the artwork?
- Does it lend a feel of activity or calm?
- What is the color temperature— warm, cool, or a mixture?
- Are there any colors that stand out in this work?
- What emotions do the colors of this work evoke?

*---> Is there continuity of shape, color, line, technique, or some other unifying element?*

*Circles*, 8" × 9" (20 × 23 cm)

## Unity and Variety

- Is the piece unified or does something look out of place and make you uncomfortable?
- Is the discomfort intentional?
- Is there repetition of some element, shape, color, or line that provides unity?
- Is there an emphasis on variety in this work?
- Is there continuity of shape, color, line, technique, or some other unifying element?

*Daffodils (wary),* 18" × 45" (46 × 114 cm)

*Black Eyed Susans (curious),* 18" × 45" (46 × 114 cm)

### The Focal Point

- Where does your eye go first, then next, and what draws it there?
- Do any lines, edges, colors, or shapes create a continuous path for your eye to follow?
- Where is the focal point placed?
- How does the focal point contrast with the other elements in the work?
- Does one thing look different from all the rest and how so?
- Is there a purposeful lack of a focal point?

--→ *What kind of balance is used?*

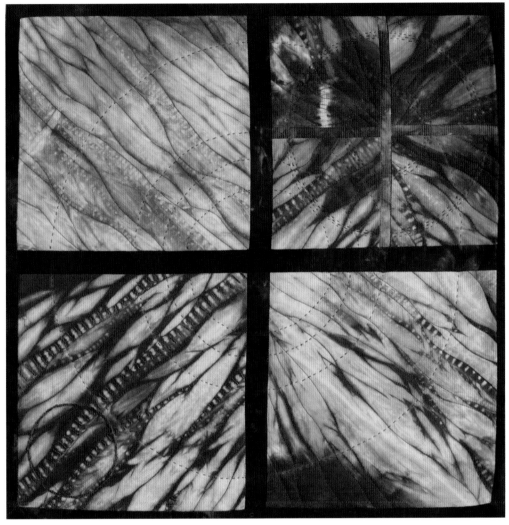

*Time,* 19" × 19" (48 × 48 cm)

## Balance and Symmetry

- What kind of balance is used—symmetrical, asymmetrical, crystallographic, or radial?
- What is the visual weight of each element and of the overall artwork?
- In what proportion are bright colors balanced with neutrals?
- Does any element in the piece strike you as unbalanced?
- Is the work deliberately unbalanced in any way?

*Malachi's Promise,* 72" × 57" (183 × 145 cm)

## Proportion and Scale

- What is the overall scale of this piece compared to human beings?
- What is the scale of each element in relation to the other elements in the piece?
- Are two different scales juxtaposed within the artwork?
- Are exaggerated internal proportions used?
- What does the scale of this work emphasize?

--→ *Are placement, size, overlap, color, and/or value shifts used to create depth?*

*Reaching,* 18" × 10" (46 × 25 cm)

## Space and Depth

- Does the artist achieve the illusion of depth or space?
- Is perspective used and do you see a vanishing point?
- Are placement, size, overlap, color, and/or value shifts used to create depth?
- Is the main subject portrayed entirely within the frame (closed form) or does it extend beyond the frame (open form)?
- How close do you appear to be to the main subject of the work?
- Is the negative space in the artwork effectively integrated?

--→ *Is there a rhythm to this piece and what does it remind you of?*

*Sisters: The Shape Of Love,* 51" × 51" (130 × 130 cm)

## Rhythm and Motion

- Is movement depicted in this work of art?
- Are angled lines contrasted with horizontal or vertical lines to enhance the illusion of motion?
- What other techniques are used to imply motion or impending motion?
- Is there a rhythm to this piece, and what does it remind you of?
- What creates the rhythm in this work?
- What single word would you use to describe the rhythm of this work?
- What elements are repeated in this work?
- Is there a progressive, alternating, or other kind of repetition used in the work?

*---> Are the techniques used appropriate to the work, and do any technical errors create a distraction?*

*Myth*, 18" × 22" (46 × 56 cm)

## Techniques and Embellishments

- Are the techniques used appropriate to the work?
- What is the dominant technique used to create this piece?
- Do any technical errors distract from the work?
- What other techniques could be used in future works like this one?
- What purpose do the embellishments serve?

- Do the embellishments add texture, shape, line, or color to the composition?
- Is the added element congruous with the rest of the quilt?
- Do the embellishments create a line or lead your eye where the artist wants it to go?
- Do the embellishments become a focal point?

# Interpretation

*To explain the meaning of the work.*

Looking at the work with your heart, answer the following questions:

---

> *Does the message touch or disturb you in any way?*

*One Nation*, 18" × 12" (46 × 30 cm)

- What is the message of the artwork?
- Does the message touch or disturb you in any way?
- Is this a literal or metaphorical piece?
- How does this work relate to current ideas or events in your world?
- How would you feel if you were inside this artwork? What is it that makes you feel that way?
- What are the expressive qualities of the work?
- What does this work remind you of?
- What memories or connotations do the materials bring to mind?

- How does the use of color influence your opinion?
- What emotions do the colors evoke and why?
- What would the impact of this artwork be with a different color scheme?
- Are there any cultural connotations intended with the use of color in this work?
- How does the balance of the work make you feel?
- How does the scale of the artwork affect your relationship with it?
- How close do you feel to the subject of the artwork?

# Questions for the Artist

*To query in order to illicit information.*

Using the following questions, evaluate the work process:

---

‑‑‑→ *What inspired this piece?*
*Did you experience any happy accidents?*

*Play With Your Food*, 18" × 27" (46 × 69 cm)

- Is this a work in progress or finished?
- What was your original intention for this piece?
- What were you thinking during the design phase?
- What happened during the decision-making process?
- What inspired this piece?
- Why did you choose these techniques?
- Why did you choose the colors in this piece?
- Did the construction process go smoothly?
- Did you experience any happy accidents?
- What was your favorite part of the process?
- What did you hope the viewer sees?
- What one thing would you change if you could?
- What is the most successful part of the piece?
- What do you think you've achieved?
- Did you learn anything new while working on this piece?
- What else has this artwork taught you?
- Will this piece lead to others, or have you said what you needed to say?

# Judgment

*To form an opinion or come to a conclusion.*

Answer these questions, or not, at the artist's discretion, remembering that these are very subjective opinions:

---→ *How original or derivative is this piece?*
*Are the techniques used for this work appropriate?*

*Mother's Hand: Magic,* 16" × 22" (41 × 56 cm)

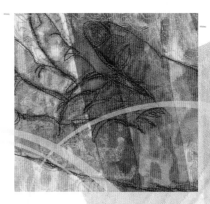

- Is the artwork successful?
- What qualities make it a success or failure?
- What is the strongest quality of the artwork?
- What is its weakest point?
- Is there anything distracting in this work?
- What criteria would you list to help others evaluate this work?
- How original or derivative is this piece?
- How does it compare with similar works?
- How does it compare to the artist's previous works?
- Can you see growth and development in the artist's work?

- How original, creative, innovative, or daring is this work?
- Are the techniques used for this work appropriate?
- Are the techniques well executed, or is there room for improvement?
- Is technique emphasized over design in this work?
- Has the artist transformed the materials?
- Does this piece function as designed?
- Would you display this work? If so, where would you display it?
- Do you prefer abstract or unusual art?
- Does the title fit?

# An Analytical Anthology

I thought you might like a few examples of valid criticisms for some of the works shown in this chapter. I don't think I've ever made a piece I thought was perfect. How could one keep on creating without being disappointed afterward? I am always able to look back and see what I could have done differently to improve each work. That does not mean that I dislike the piece. In fact, some of the works that have the greatest design problems or technical issues are favorites of mine. The love of art is, after all, subjective. Remember also, that your judgments might be entirely different from mine and equally valid. Refer to the pages noted to see the entire piece.

*The Women Of God Know This*, see page 108

*Malachi's Promise*, see page 116

Successes: The crispness of the lettering and photograph cropping. I also love the grandmother's face in this piece.

Lessons learned: I would have left out the fingers on grandmothers shoulder—another photo editing decision. Faces are difficult, but I continue to improve.

Successes: The curve of the tree and its shading are exactly what I was looking for. The family portraits in the border blend perfectly and are often only noticed on close inspection.

Lessons learned: I worked for ages to collage and print individual faces of our ancestors onto organza to create the two large faces. There is so little value contrast in them that nobody knows they are there unless it is pointed out. I also would have raised the woman's face so her chin and neck are not buried in the landscape.

*Three Leaves*, see page 107

*Sisters: The Shape Of Love,* see page 118

Successes: The complementary blue makes the oranges sing. The circular quilted lines are subtle but lend balance to the busy lower left corner.

Lessons learned: You don't have to go with your first idea. This is a second iteration of a design that wasn't working.

Successes: The peaceful cool analogous color scheme and the watery flow of the words.

Lesson learned: Edit your photos. This is a favorite picture of my sisters and me lying on each other's shoulders. Viewers are confused by the two directions the heads face.

*Black Eyed Susans (curious)*, see page 114

*Stone, Water, Time*, see page 111

Successes: I painted the cables green after the pieces were quilted. Scary, but they added just the right frame for the figures. I love the tiny fairy—an adaption of a photo of my youngest daughter.

Lessons learned: Painting figures takes time to learn, and I still haven't figured out how to quilt them without losing the smoothness of the skin. I might have added a daffodil bud at the bottom of "Black-eyed Susan" to balance the color.

Successes: The element of line in this work is pleasing to me, with a variety of weights and directions. This continues to be a favorite of mine, especially after adding the kanji (several years after the piece was "finished") for the words Stone, Water, and Time.

Lessons learned: Before the kanji, this piece had a horizontal orientation. I think, for most Western sensibilities, having the visual weight of the piece hovering at the top leaves most viewers uncomfortable.

*Place,* see page 110

*Reaching,* see page 117

Successes: I like the textural quilting in the background of this piece and the mix of materials, one of my first experiments with mixing paper and cloth.

Lessons learned: Something about the bar on the right is throwing off the balance of the piece. The piece began with a strip of my favorite shibori-dyed fabric, and perhaps I was too in love with the materials to listen to the piece tell me it wasn't needed there anymore.

Successes: The sphere is painted in, and I was happy with the blending of the paint into the texture of the mottled hand-dyed fabric. I like the depth and dimension that the dark against the light creates.

Lessons learned: The focal point is too centered for my taste. I might go in and add some interesting symbols down the left side of the piece to add a weight and a little more asymmetry.

*Myth*, see page 119

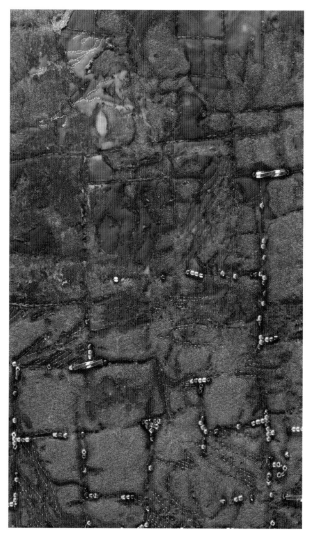

*Rust*, page 109

Successes: I enjoy the subtle color shifts layered behind the burnt-away organza in this piece. The focal point, one area with less texture than the rest of the piece, gives the eye a place to rest. The mysterious "letters" give the viewer something to question and wonder about.

Lessons learned: This piece was made for an exhibit called the PAQA Post Project that consisted of imaginary postage stamps. The scalloped border doesn't make much sense when the piece is taken out of context.

Successes: The overall texture is exactly what I was looking for, and the beaded embellishments are well integrated into the design of the piece.

Lessons learned: There is no resting place for the eye, no real focal point, leading the viewer to lose interest quickly in this piece. I might add a much greater amount of beads, creating more of a path for the eye to follow, if not a blatant focal point.

*Mother's Hand: Magic*, see page 122

*Mother's Hand: Burnt Out*, see page 112

Successes: The red hand is well drawn and I like the way it fades into the piece. This was a happy accident when I melted part of the red synthetic chiffon it was made of. I also like the color scheme.

Lessons learned: There are three small hands being juggled in the air—they don't have enough contrast to be noticed. Perhaps a heavier outline in red and carefully placed beads would give them more emphasis.

Successes: I think the technique is perfectly suited to the message of this quilt (dealing with postpartum depression.) There's good color contrast achieved by layering the burnt-out top quilt with a complementary-colored back quilt.

Lesson learned: Again, the small hands on the bottom right corner lack enough contrast to show well.

*Time,* page 115

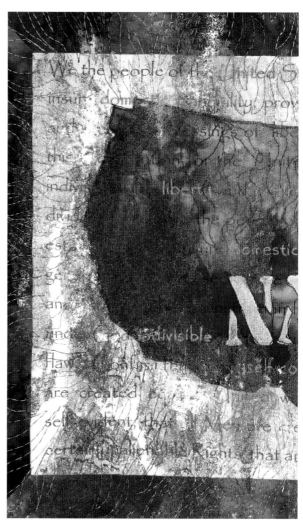

*One Nation,* see page 120

Successes: This continues to be one of my favorites. The weight and the variation of lines are pleasing to me.

Lessons learned: The balance is off, and I continue to rotate the piece trying to fix it. I wonder what would happen if it was broken into four separate squares, each being wrapped on stretcher bars and arranged in a horizontal line?

Successes: The partially obscured lettering conveyed the emotion I was looking for, frustration at the violent backlash many Muslim-Americans experienced after the tragic events of 9/11. I am also very happy with the quilting stitches in the border.

Lesson learned: I had a great time learning new techniques, such as sending fabric through a laser printer.

*Play With Your Food,* see page 121

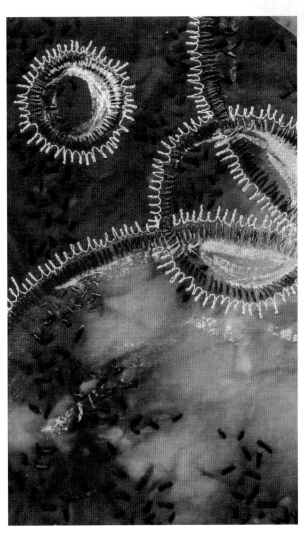

*Circles,* page 113

Successes: This is a playful piece, printed with actual slices of fruit—including squishy bananas! I like the symmetry and the whimsy of one odd-color pear.

Lessons learned: It is easy to let a border print overpower the main focus of the piece in a more traditional "quilt-like" setting. I might need to add a heavier outline to the fruits.

Successes: I really like the texture of this piece with the heavily embroidered red circles and the seed stitching.

Lessons learned: I'm not sure the gold paint added anything to the composition. I would, however, like to continue to explore the idea of embroidered and overlapping circles.

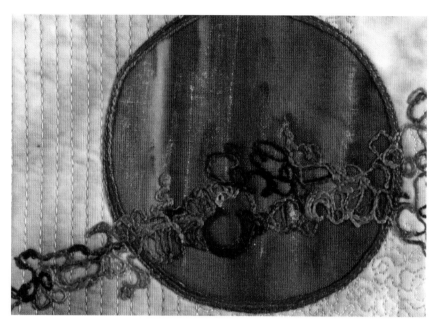

*Untitled Small Work,* page 106

Successes: I like the overall composition, texture, and direction of line of this piece.

Lessons learned: Presentation matters. The piece is mounted on Plexiglas, a very interesting treatment, but it allows for too much interaction between the piece and the color of the wall it is hung on. This work might be better presented on an interestingly painted gallery-wrapped canvas.

# Conclusion

Well, here we are at the end of our current journey. Have you enjoyed this adventure?

Hopefully, you've worked through the exercises and come to a better understanding of the elements and principles that make up the letters and words in the language of visual art. Paying attention to and analyzing how other artists use these tools will help you to more successfully use them in your own work. You may have found that some concepts come easily to you, but others require a little time and perspiration. Good—now you know where to concentrate more of your effort in the future. (Of course, I mean on the element that is most difficult for you to grasp!)

I appreciate your willingness to share this path with me. The road to becoming an artist is certainly an interesting one. It isn't a destination but a never ending journey with many fascinating points of interest along the way. Sometimes we thunder down the road on a galloping horse; other times we kick and curse like a stubborn old mule.

With each new work, we need to learn what we can from it, then give our baby a kiss good-bye and send it off into the world to see how it will fare. Don't see the success or failure of a piece for sale or being juried for a prestigious show as a reflection of your skill. Just let it go! Really— a piece that's rejected from one show might win an award in the next.

The important thing is to keep working, to keep learning how to express yourself visually. Your fluency in the language of art will slowly but surely, become more eloquent. With time and effort, you will create visual poetry.

# Index

# Create inspiring designs
## with these resources from Interweave

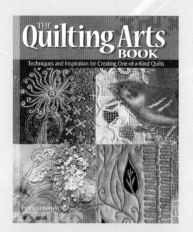